WHISPERS of the HEART

*Exploring the Silent Struggles
of Women Through Christian Counselling
and Family Therapy*

DR. OLIVIA WINNER, PHD (HC)

Whispers of the Heart: *Exploring the Silent Struggles of Women Through Christian Counselling and Family Therapy*
By **Dr. Olivia Winner, PhD HC**

Published in the United Kingdom by **Yonda Limited Publishing**
Yonda Limited
Suite 119, 7-8 New Road Avenue, Chatham, Kent ME4 6BB

Artistic Illustrations © Moses, Mikel and Michelle Winner

The right of Dr. Olivia Winner to be identified as the author and illustrator of this work has been asserted in accordance with the Copyright, Designs and Patents Act 1988.

All rights reserved. No part of this publication may be reproduced, stored in a retrieval system, or transmitted in any form or by any means; electronic, mechanical, photocopying, recording, or otherwise, without prior written permission of the publisher, except in the case of brief quotations used in reviews, articles or other non-commercial uses permitted by copyright law.

For permission requests, please contact the publisher at:
Permission Coordinator
Email: Info@yondalimited.com

This book is sold subject to the condition that it shall not, by way of trade or otherwise, be lent, resold, hired out, or circulated in any form other than that in which it is published and without a similar condition being imposed on the subsequent purchaser.

Disclaimer
This is a work of non-fiction. Some names and identifying details have been changed to protect the privacy of individuals. All stories, case studies and personal examples are shared with appropriate permissions or are fictionalised composites, used respectfully and for illustrative purposes only.

This is a work of non-fiction. Some names and identifying details have been changed to protect the privacy of individuals. Case studies, personal stories and examples are shared with permission or are fictionalised composites, included respectfully for illustrative purposes only.

Unless otherwise indicated, all Scripture quotations are taken from the **Holy Bible, New International Version® (NIV®)**. Copyright © 1973, 1978, 1984, 2011 by Biblica, Inc.™ Used by permission. All rights reserved worldwide.

For more information, permissions, or speaking engagements, contact:
Winners Female Family Organization

First Printing Edition: September 2025
Cover Design Concept: Moses, Mikel, and Michelle Winner
Editorial Support: Yonda Limited (www.yondalimited.com)
Book Design: Nonon Tech & Design

ISBN: 978-1-0369-3588-7

WHISPERS of the HEART

Dedication

To every woman who has ever smiled through sorrow and carried burdens too heavy for words- this book is for you.

To every daughter raised in cultures where silence was mistaken for strength

To the wives who were told to submit even when it cost them their joy

To the mothers whose bodies carried pain unspoken, from menstruation to menopause.

To the widows and single women made invisible by church and society

To the friend who has carried hidden pain and wondered if God sees.

This book is for you.

And to my daughters and sons: may you grow in a world where honesty is welcomed, dignity is protected and silence no longer hides suffering.

May your voice be heard, your healing begin and your identity be restored in Christ.

Above all, the One who sees all, heals all, and loves without measure- Jesus Christ, my Redeemer and Counsellor.

TABLE OF CONTENTS

Acknowledgements 1

Foreword (HRH Queen Dr. Nana Adjoa Akyekumaa I) 3

Preface: The Inaudible Voice 5

Author's Introduction: Behind the Curtain of Silence 9

Scriptural Reflection: Scriptural Truths that Heal 15

Devotional Prayer 17

Reader's Note: How to Use This Book 19

Part One: The Hidden Life of Women 23

Chapter One: The Mask of Strength: When resilience conceals pain 25

Chapter Two: Taboo Seasons: Menstruation and Menopause 33

Chapter Three: Unseen Illnesses: Endometriosis, PCOS, Fibroids and Fibromyalgia 39

Chapter Four: The Quiet Mind: Anxiety, Depression, ADHD and Postnatal struggles 45

Part Two: Silence in Relationships and Systems 51

Chapter Five: Behind Closed Doors:
Abuse in Christian homes 53

Chapter Six: Twisted Teachings:
When submission becomes suppression 59

Chapter Seven: The Invisible Load:
Emotional labour and unshared responsibility 67

Chapter Eight: Workplace Wounds:
Microaggressions, motherhood penalty, discrimination............73

Chapter Nine: The Shadow of Shame:
Cultural and spiritual weight of secrecy..79

Chapter Ten: Bodies Under Scrutiny –
Infertility, miscarriage, abortion and judgement 85

Chapter Eleven: Trauma That Lingers:
Violence, coercion, and cultural silencing......................................93

Part Three: Women Carrying Public and Private Roles 101

Chapter Twelve: The Lonely Leader –
Isolation at the top... 103

Chapter Thirteen: Behind the Pulpit Wife's Smile:
Ministry marriages under pressure 109

Chapter Fourteen: Motherhood's Quiet Fears:
The hidden weight of raising children... 115

Chapter Fifteen: Faith Under Fire:
Spiritual doubt and silence in Christian life................................ 121

Part Four: Seasons of Womanhood **127**

    Chapter Sixteen: Single, Not Silent:
    Misconceptions about unmarried women 129

    Chapter Seventeen: Widows in the Shadows:
    Grief, invisibility and resilience 135

    Chapter Eighteen: Growing Older, Growing Stronger:
    Ageing and the fear of irrelevance 141

    Chapter Nineteen: Daughters Under Pressure:
    Young women in a digital age 147

    Chapter Twenty: When the Church is Silent:
    Failures of faith communities to protect women 153

Part Five: Breaking Silence, Finding Wholeness **159**

    Chapter Twenty-One: Breaking Silence:
    Finding Wholeness 161

Epilogue: Let the Silence Be Broken 167

Closing Devotional Prayer – From Silence to Healing 172

Glossary of Key Terms 173

Bibliography 179

Scripture Index 185

About the Author 189

ACKNOWLEDGEMENTS

I give thanks to God, who has been my refuge, strength, and source of wisdom throughout this journey. Without His guidance, this book would never have taken shape.

To my husband and children, thank you for your patience, love and encouragement as I poured my heart and time into writing. Your presence grounds me and reminds me why breaking silence matters.

To the women who entrusted me with their stories, whether in counselling rooms, church pews, or private conversations, you are the heartbeat of this book. Though your names are protected, your voices echo here.

To my community of faith, mentors, and friends in both Uganda and the UK, thank you for your prayers, listening ears, and gentle nudges to keep writing when I doubted my voice.

Finally, to every reader who picks up this book: thank you for opening your heart to hear what so many women have long carried quietly.

FOREWORD
(HRH Queen Dr. Nana Adjoa Akyekumaa I)

It is with deep admiration and a profound sense of purpose that I pen this foreword for Whispers of the Heart, a powerful and deeply moving work by Dr. Olivia Winner, a woman of unshakable faith, compassion and vision.

In a world where the silent struggles of women often go unheard and unacknowledged, Dr. Winner has taken up the noble mantle of advocacy and healing. Through this book, she opens a sacred space for the hidden voices of countless women who carry their pain in silence. Drawing from her wealth of experience in Christian counselling and family therapy, she gently guides the reader through themes of trauma, resilience, spiritual restoration and emotional freedom.

As President and Founder of the Winner Female Family Organization, Dr. Olivia Winner is not just an author or therapist; she is a beacon for communities. Her organization gives voice to the voiceless, strength to the broken and dignity to those who have long been forgotten. This book is a natural extension of her life's work and mission.

Whispers of the Heart is more than a publication; it is a ministry. It reminds us all that healing is possible and that God still speaks through the brokenhearted. I encourage every reader to engage with these pages not only with open eyes but with an open heart. Let this work inspire you to listen more deeply and lift others more boldly.

HRH Queen DR. Nana Adjoa Akyekumaa I
Development Queen Mother
Gomoa Abonko - Gyease Division of Gomoa Assin Traditional Area.

PREFACE

The Inaudible Voice

> ❝
> *There is a time to be silent and a time to speak.*
> - ECCLESIASTES 3:7
> ❞

There is a particular kind of pain that does not scream. It carries no dramatic gestures and no visible wounds. Instead it lingers, subtle, constant and often unnamed. It shows up in the sigh at the sink, the smile that never reaches the eyes, the polite *"I'm fine"* that hides a storm.

This is the pain of many women.

Over the years, in therapy rooms, prayer meetings, hospital corridors, and church pews, I have encountered this quiet grief more times than I can count. It is the ache of women who feel dismissed, overlooked, and unheard not because their suffering isn't real but because it does not fit the narratives we are comfortable with.

As a woman of faith and a Christian counsellor, I have wrestled deeply with the role silence plays in women's lives. Not all silence is harmful. There is a silence that is sacred: stillness before God, the quiet space where reflection and renewal take place. But there is also a silence that suffocates. The silence born of fear, shame, or cultural expectation. A silence mistaken for obedience but in truth the residue of trauma.

This book is a response to that kind of silence. It seeks to name the unnamed and bring to light issues too often left hidden because they are uncomfortable. These chapters are not exhaustive, nor do they claim to be a definitive guide to womanhood. They are invitations to reflect, to question, to feel and ultimately, to speak. They are shaped by clinical experience, scriptural reflection and above all, the lived stories of women: women battling silently with invisible illness, unjust expectations, emotional abuse and reproductive grief.

My prayer is that here you will find language for your own journey and that leaders, carers, and friends will grow in sensitivity and compassion because what we do not talk about, we cannot heal and what we do not heal, we end up passing on.

May this book be a beginning not an end, a first conversation not the last.

Let the silence end here.

Note on stories and Case Reflections: *Some stories are shared with permission; others are composites to protect confidentiality. Names and details have been changed to honour dignity while conveying truth.*

AUTHOR'S INTRODUCTION:

Behind the Curtain of Silence

Women across the United Kingdom and indeed across the globe live through daily struggles that rarely see the light of day. These are not the stories splashed across headlines or trending hashtags. They are not debated in parliament or broadcast in primetime news. They live instead in hushed conversations behind closed doors, in silent tears cried in office toilets, in battles fought in doctors' surgeries often alone and dismissed.

Drawing from my professional background; holding a PhD in Christian counselling and specialising in families and child therapy, I have witnessed first- hand the profound impact that unspoken emotional and psychological burdens can have on women and their loved ones. These hidden issues do not remain confined to the individual; they ripple through marriages, children, churches and communities, often perpetuating cycles of pain and misunderstanding.

This book seeks to uncover the mental, emotional and spiritual struggles. Whether it is the grinding weight of emotional labour, the cruel invisibility of chronic pain, or the subtle suffocation of cultural and religious expectation, the issues explored here are deeply familiar to many women yet scarcely acknowledged in public discourse. My hope is that women will be seen, their pain acknowledged, and their healing begun. This is not a book of despair but of deliverance rooted in the living hope of Christ.

My journey: Called to Listen, Compelled to Speak

I did not arrive at these insights merely through books, academic lectures or theological debates; though all have shaped me. I came to them by listening. Listening to women whisper what they could not say aloud at home. Listening to children trying to make sense of an emotionally absent mother. Listening to well-meaning but bewildered husbands, friends with women in their lives that they loved but whose pain they could not name.

As a Christian counsellor with a doctorate in counselling, marriage, families and child therapy, I have spent countless hours in that sacred space where vulnerability meets truth. Therapy is both psychology and spiritual practice. It is the place where confession meets compassion, where burdens are shared, and where the soul can rest after carrying what no one else could see.

I pursued this path out of academic curiosity and out of conviction: a deep, unshakable sense that women are carrying more than their share of hidden burdens and too often. Their silence is mistaken for strength. My faith calls me to see every person as an image-bearer of God. Yet I have seen how cultural systems, church structures and family expectations blur that image in a woman's own eyes.

The Collision of Silence and Shame

Over the years, I have witnessed how silence and shame collide, particularly in Christian communities.
- Women with depression were told to "pray more."
- Those in emotionally abusive marriages were urged to "submit and be patient."
- Mothers grieving the loss of a child were offered shallow assurances that "God has a plan."

For years, I sat across from women who spoke confidently in public but cried in silence. Women who raised families, led businesses, served faithfully in their churches, and yet felt unseen in their deepest pain. These were not weak women but they were strong women carrying hidden wounds. Some had never been given permission to speak. Others did not even know they had a voice.

Faith when rooted in love and truth liberates but when distorted, it imprisons. My work has been to help disentangle those threads to walk with women as they rediscover their worth, voice and their agency as individuals and as daughters in the body of Christ.

Professional and Personal

This book is both professional and personal.
- Professional because it draws on years of counselling practice, clinical insight and academic training shaped by biblical compassion and psychological precision.
- Personal because as a woman, wife, mother, and believer, I have walked through seasons of silence and know the cost of carrying unspoken wounds. Silence is not always peace but it is often pain unspoken, shame unhealed and trauma unnamed. Faith gives us hope but it does not erase our humanity. God never asked us to hide our hurt. He invites us to bring it to Him.

An Invitation

I write for the woman of faith who feels her pain is too small to matter, the mother who feels invisible, the daughter who has never been heard and the leader who smiles in public but weeps in private.

I write because I have listened and so that you might feel heard.

This book is not only a clinical reflection or a theological discussion. It is a compassionate invitation to uncover the quiet struggles so that many women carry and to move toward healing. Within these pages you will find stories of real women, scriptural wisdom and therapeutic insight woven together so that you may feel seen, understood and free.

My prayer is that as you read, you will find yourself in these words and also find your voice, your value and victory. This is your time to move from silence to healing, from shame to significance and from brokenness to beauty.

May God who sees, hears and loves you, walk with you through every chapter of this journey with grace and compassion.

Dr. Olivia Winner
PhD in Christian Counselling, Marriage, Families and Child Therapy.
The Winners Female Family Organization.

SCRIPTURAL REFLECTION

Scriptural Truths that Heal

> *You are the God who sees me.*
> - GENESIS 16:13 (NIV)

Long before women had voices in courts, pulpits, or parliaments, Scripture recorded the cry of a single, suffering woman, Hagar. She was cast out, used and misunderstood. By all accounts her story might have been lost in the margins of history but God met her, not in a palace, not in a temple but in the wilderness.

It was in that barren place, when her pain could no longer be hidden and her future seemed impossible, that Hagar gave God a name: *El Roi, "the God who sees me."* Not just the God who sees everything, but the God who sees me. The God who notices the overlooked. The God who bends down to the prayers whispered in tents, toilets, or therapy rooms. The God who honours tears shed in silence.

This is the heart of the gospel for women who suffer quietly. While society tells women to be strong, to carry on and to keep quiet, Scripture assures us that even in the wilderness, God sees, listens and acts.

Jesus embodied this truth. He noticed the woman with the issue of blood who reached out to touch Him in secret, and He called her *"Daughter."* He defended the woman caught in adultery, silencing her accusers with the words, "Neither do I condemn you." He honoured the woman who knelt and wept at His feet, pouring out her grief in tears instead of words.

He did not silence them. He dignified them.

So if you have felt unheard, dismissed, or shamed, let this be your reminder: silence does not disqualify you from divine attention. God sees, knows and has always made room at his table for the woman whose pain was too complex, too hidden, or too inconvenient for others.

DEVOTIONAL PRAYER

This book is written in the spirit of Hagar's declaration: *El Roi- God who sees*. Not God who sees only perfection or performance but God who sees your unseen work, private pain and your quiet resilience.

Before the first chapter begins, let that be your anchor.

You are seen.
You are known.
You are not alone.

A Prayer for the Unseen

Loving and Compassionate God.
You who see the depths of our hearts.
You who know the pain that no one else perceives.
We come before You now.
not with loud cries but with silent sighs.
not with bold declarations but with trembling hope.

For the woman who wakes tired and worn.
For the mother who feels invisible.
For the daughter who carries wounds too deep for words.
For the sister whose faith feels fragile.
You see them all Lord and know them all.

We ask for Your gentle presence to surround each weary soul. May Your peace which surpasses all understanding guard their hearts and minds.
May Your strength uphold them when their own falters.
May Your love remind them that silence is not loneliness and that in their weaknesses your power is made perfect.

Help us God to break the chains of shame.
To speak truth where silence has reigned too long.
To bear one another's burdens with grace and courage.
Teach us to listen without judgement.
To comfort without words and to love as you love us fully and unconditionally.

In the quiet places be our refuge.
In hidden sorrows be our healing.
In the unseen struggles be our ever- present help.

May this book be a companion on their journey, a lantern in the dark and a reminder of Your unending love.

In Jesus' mighty name! Amen.

READER'S NOTE:

How to Use This Book

> ❝ *This book of the law shall not depart from your mouth, but you shall meditate on it day and night.*
> *- JOSHUA 1:8* ❞

This is not a book to skim quickly or consume in a single sitting. It is an invitation to pause, listen, and engage both your own story and God's in new ways.

Each chapter has been written with care to help you move gently but intentionally from silence toward healing. Within the pages you will find:

- Live Stories drawn from counselling and pastoral encounters shared to help you recognise yourself or those you love.
- Biblical Reflections that root these struggles in God's Word reminding us that He sees and speaks into every hidden pain.

- Counselling Insights offering practical tools for growth, resilience and wholeness.
- Reflection & Discussion Guides at the end of each chapter with prompts for journaling, prayer or small group conversations. Use them honestly and allow them to guide you into deeper dialogue with God and the trusted community.
- Scripture Reflections for the Reader anchoring you in God's promises with verses to meditate on in your personal devotion.

How you use this book is up to you:
- You may choose to read it straight through, treating the book as a journey.
- You may prefer to sit slowly with one chapter at a time whilst journaling your reflections.
- You may wish to gather with a group of women, counsellors, or church leaders using the guides for collective healing and discussion.

Above all, read prayerfully and bring your story into dialogue with what you encounter here, cry if you need to, question if you must, mark the pages, write in the margins and invite the Holy Spirit to meet you in the process.

This is a book of information and transformation written so that silence may be broken, shame dismantled and healing embraced.

List of Abbreviations
- **ADHD** - Attention Deficit Hyperactivity Disorder
- **PCOS** - Polycystic Ovary Syndrome
- **PTSD** - Post-Traumatic Stress Disorder
- **NIV** – New International Version (Bible translation)
- **NRSV** – New Revised Standard Version (Bible translation, if you quote it)
- **ESV** – English Standard Version (Bible translation, if you quote it)
- **WHO** – World Health Organization (you reference in Bibliography)
- **EHRC** – Equality and Human Rights Commission (UK, in Bibliography)
- **ONS** – Office for National Statistics (UK, in Bibliography)
- **DSM-5** – Diagnostic and Statistical Manual of Mental Disorders, Fifth Edition
- **BMJ** – British Medical Journal
- **NGO** – Non-Governmental Organization (if referenced in cultural/legal contexts)
- **AI** – Artificial Intelligence (if referenced in modern workplace/tech sections)
- **U.K. / U.S.** – United Kingdom / United States

PART ONE:
The Hidden Life of Women

Women often carry wounds that never show on the surface. This section uncovers the inner struggles, masked strength, taboo seasons of the body, invisible illnesses and quiet battles of the mind that remain unseen but deeply felt.

CHAPTER ONE

The Mask of Strength:
When resilience conceals pain

> ❝
> Even in laughter the heart may ache and
> the end of joy may be grief.
> - PROVERBS 14:13
> ❞

Some women learn to survive by smiling through sorrow. This chapter explores how masks of strength protect in public yet corrode in private and why honesty is the first step toward healing.

1. The Precious Gift of Womanhood

A woman is first recognised at birth as female, bearing the biological design of two X chromosomes, and with it the potential to carry children. Menstruation, a monthly rhythm of the body, marks her distinction from men and shapes her path through life.

Across cultures, the arrival of a girl child is celebrated in ways that carry meaning far beyond the moment. In many

African communities, elders gather to name the child with words of blessing, invoking strength, beauty and continuity of family. In parts of Asia, families give red eggs or choose names with careful attention to character and destiny. In the Netherlands, neighbours mark the street with decorations to welcome her. These rituals remind us that womanhood is viewed as a gift to family and society.

The Bible echoes this value. Women such as Ruth, Esther and Mary Magdalene carried courage, faith and leadership in moments that changed history. They remind us that a woman is not only precious but powerful in God's story.

However, for many the joy celebrated at birth gives way to years of masked pain. The girl who was once named with hope learns, as she grows, to hide her sorrow behind strength.

2. When the Smile Lies

In the counselling room, I have often sat with women whose smiles were flawless, whose words sounded confident, whose faith appeared unshaken. Yet their eyes told a different story. Behind the warmth was exhaustion, behind the smile and polite conversation was a quiet heart breaking filled with trauma, disappointment, rejection and despair.

Many of us learn this performance early. Whilst in Christian spaces the pressure is greater, Joy is equated with holiness and lament is seen as a weakness. So women raise their hands in worship, quote scripture, and serve faithfully all the while carrying grief or abuse they dare not name.

A smile can be a mask for survival. It shields us from judgement, misunderstanding or the accusation of being *"weak in faith." Proverbs 14:13* reminds us that *"even in laughter the heart may ache."*

This journey is to bring healing through truth, freedom through honesty and hope through Christ- centered counsel. You are not alone. God is not afraid of your wounds, He intends to heal them.

3. The Mask of Strength: Why we Hide

Some communities interpret the Bible's teaching on submission to mean that a woman must always remain silent when men are expressing their views and in some cases this right is abused.

1 Peter 3:1–3 (NIV).
1. Wives in the same way be submissive to their husbands so that if any of them do not believe the word, they may be won over without words by the behaviour of their wives.
2. When they see the purity and reverence of your lives.
3. Your beauty should not come from outward adornment, such as braided hair and the wearing of gold jewelry and fine clothes.

The Good News Bible addresses the submission of wives in marriage without detailing the extent to which that right can be abused. In many marriages, particularly in Sub- Saharan Africa, mutual respect and honour are the guiding principles yet when these are absent, submission can be distorted into control.

In my own Ugandan upbringing, we were taught to "be strong, you are a woman." We learned early that showing emotion could be unsafe or unwanted especially in environments where vulnerability is misunderstood as a weakness. Over time, this conditioning became internalised. Emotional honesty became a risk. Pain had to be managed, concealed or spiritualised. Strength became less a gift and more a burden.

In churches this struggle becomes even more complex and the pressure deepens. Well- meaning but harmful words "just pray more," or "don't claim that pain", leave women with the idea that spiritual maturity is incompatible with emotional struggle. This creates a culture of secrecy and suppression. Instead of confessing our wounds, we curate an image of victory, smile to hide and polish our appearance instead of seeking healing.

God sees past the mask. Scripture tells us of David weeping in the *Psalms*, Job cursing the day of his birth *(Job 3-5 NIV)* and Jesus Himself sweating blood in Gethsemane *(Luke 22: 44)* and crying out in anguish *"My God, why have You forsaken Me?" (Matthew 27:46)*. These accounts remind us that pain does not disqualify faith. God welcomes honesty and not performance.

4. Case Reflection: A Story Behind the Smile

Martha (a composite story shared with permission) came to me in the counselling room dressed impeccably, her hair neat, her smile radiant. She was a deacon's wife, admired as a leader in her church. On the outside she looked composed; inside she was unravelling her voice trembled.

"I don't think I can do this anymore," she finally whispered.

Her husband's family neglected her emotions and criticised her for having "ugly" single- sex children. They exchanged whispered complaints about her overstaying at church and neglecting her household duties. Church members expected her to give endlessly without rest. For years she smiled through her exhaustion and chronic anxiety, believing strength was her duty but in private she cried herself to sleep, empty and afraid.

Her healing began when she dared to be honest before God, before a counsellor, and eventually before her community. When she was seen not as a leader or role model but as a woman in need of care, the path to restoration opened.

5. The Cost of Pretending

There is an English saying: *If you close your eyes because bad people are passing, you will never see the good people passing.* In other words, presence has no room in life if we shut ourselves off from it.

Pretence takes many forms. The schoolgirl who hides menstrual struggles for fear of teasing. The Christian wife who smiles through worship without ever revealing the pain she endures on her marital bed. The mother who never admits her depression.

The Bible tells of Hannah, who carried silent anguish in her polygamous marriage until one day, seeking desire for a more meaningful union with her husband, she cried openly before God. Those around her misunderstood but God heard and responded. When wounds remain hidden, healing is delayed. Suppressed pain often resurfaces as anxiety, anger, addiction or relational conflict.

Pretending also weakens spiritual intimacy. The Book of Psalms shows us that worship and honesty are not opposites but companions. God does not ask for polished prayers rather He asks for the truth. Masks may fool people but never Him.

6. The Healing Path: From Hiding to Honesty

Healing begins when we give ourselves permission to be real. In the presence of Christ, there is no need for disguise. He welcomes the weary, grieving and the broken.

Practical steps on this path:
- Name the wound. Speak plainly before God. Say what hurts.
- Seek safe company. Wise counsellors, trusted friends or faith leaders can hold space for truth.
- Embrace lament. Tears, questions, even silence are part of prayer.
- Release performance. You are not your strength or your service but you are God's beloved.

Closing Thought

The mask of strength often begins in childhood and is reinforced in faith spaces that prize performance over lament but the smile that hides your wounds does not disqualify you from God's love.

God sees beyond the surface and welcomes you just as you are; weary, wounded and longing for rest. Tears, questions and confession belong in prayer and community. True healing begins not with pretending to be strong but with the courage to be honest before Him and with those who care for you. Be encouraged and know that your tears are not wasted; they are noticed, recorded, and cherished by the One who binds up the broken-hearted. Let your smile become testimony, not camouflage.

> "You keep track of all my sorrows. You have collected all my tears in your bottle. You have recorded each one in your book"
> - PSALM 56:8

Reflection & Discussion

1. What pain have I hidden behind a smile?
2. How have family, culture, or church shaped the way I express or suppress emotions?
3. What might honesty before God and trusted others look like in my life today?

Scripture for Meditation

- "He heals the broken-hearted and binds up their wounds." - Psalm 147:3.
- "Come to Me, all you who are weary and burdened, and I will give you rest." - Matthew 11:28.
- "My grace is sufficient for you, for My power is made perfect in weakness." - 2 Corinthians 12:9.

CHAPTER TWO

Taboo Seasons: Menstruation and Menopause

> **"**
> *I praise you because I am fearfully and wonderfully made.*
> – PSALM 139:14
> **"**

Cycles of womanhood are part of God's design, yet churches and cultures often shroud them in silence. Here we break the taboos that leave women unprepared and unsupported through these natural transitions.

1. The Silence Around Women's Cycles

Menstruation and menopause shape the lives of women everywhere, yet both remain shrouded in silence. In many homes they are treated as private matters to be endured quietly. In churches they are rarely mentioned as if female biology does not belong in conversations of faith.

From the moment a girl begins her period, she learns quickly what is acceptable to speak of and what must be hidden. Too often, her body's natural rhythm is met with embarrassment or shame. By the time she reaches midlife that silence extends to menopause. What should be acknowledged as a natural transition becomes something whispered about if spoken of at all.

This silence is not harmless. It leaves women unprepared, unsupported and spiritually isolated at key points in their lives.

This chapter examines how misinformation, systemic neglect and cultural silence surrounding the female biological cycle contribute to emotional distress and spiritual confusion. It also offers a Christian counselling response one rooted in Scripture, psychology and pastoral care.

2. Menstruation: A Quiet Burden

Menstruation is the monthly shedding of the uterine lining, an ordinary biological process that allows the possibility of new life. Yet many girls grow up treating it as a source of shame rather than a sign of God's design.

In parts of Sub-Saharan Africa, schoolgirls often miss classes because of inadequate sanitation facilities or poverty that makes sanitary products unaffordable. The experience is given little consideration, instead it is treated as "business as usual," even though it can significantly affect a girl's performance. In many Christian families across the world, menstruation is not explained, leaving generations of daughters to navigate their reproductive years unprepared, ashamed or confused, often internalising negative messages about their worth and their bodies. A subject that should be spoken of with reverence is covered instead with silence, embarrassment or neglect.

For women in the workplace, menstruation can bring challenges that are met with little understanding. Pain or fatigue is dismissed as exaggeration. Taking time off may be seen as a weakness. Even in Christian leadership, women often feel the need to hide what they are experiencing so that their faith is not questioned.

3. Menopause: The Unspoken Transition

Menopause the natural decline of reproductive hormones usually beginning around midlife is a transition every woman will eventually face. Symptoms such as hot flushes, mood changes and commonly vaginal dryness which can cause discomfort in marital intimacy. Few women find safe spaces to speak about these challenges.

Too often, menopause is treated as a decline rather than a new season of life. Women are left to wrestle with their changing bodies and shifting identities alone. In Christian communities, the silence can be especially heavy. Some women fear being judged as less capable or less spiritual if they admit their struggles. Others endure in silence believing this is the godly way.

Yet scripture reminds us: *"To everything there is a season and a time for every purpose under heaven" (Ecclesiastes 3:1)*. Menopause is not a shameful decline but part of God's rhythm for the body.

4. The Wound of Dismissal: Medical Gaslighting and Emotional Invalidity

Many women encounter what is now called medical gaslighting, it is the practice of dismissing or downplaying a patient's symptoms. A woman who speaks of debilitating cramps is told it is *"just part of being a woman."* Another raising concerns about premenopause may be told she is overreacting.

This dismissal compounds suffering. Not only is she battling the symptoms of her body but she is also battling the disbelief of those she turns to for help. Spiritually, this can shake confidence. If her voice is not heard by those entrusted to care for her, she may begin to doubt her worth.

The Gospel reminds us of the woman who had bled for twelve years. Society pushed her to the margins, yet Jesus stopped, listened and restored her publicly: *"Daughter, your faith has made you well" (Luke 8:48)*. Christ did not ignore her pain. He dignified it.

5. A Pastoral Response

As Christian counsellors, leaders, and carers, we are called to bring voice where silence has reigned. To do this we must:

- **Name the silence.** Speak of menstruation and menopause openly without shame. Give women the language they have lacked.
- **Educate and equip.** Challenge myths and create space in families, churches and workplaces for accurate teaching and compassionate conversation.
- **Ground in scripture.** Affirm that these cycles are not curses but part of God's design. They are seasons of life not signs of failure.
- **Lead with empathy.** Mirror the posture of Jesus who never dismissed female suffering but healed it with honour.

Closing Thought

Menstruation and menopause are not marginal matters. They are milestones in a woman's life that shape her body, her relationships and her faith. When met with silence or shame, they wound deeply. When approached with truth and compassion, they can become seasons of dignity and grace.

As a community of faith, we must do more than pray for women in these transitions. We must listen, honour our bodies as temples of the Holy Spirit and remind them that God's presence does not waver through any stage of life.

Reflection & Discussion

1. What messages about menstruation or menopause shaped your view of your body?
2. Have you experienced dismissal or shame in these areas? How has it affected your faith?
3. How can Christian families, churches, and workplaces create safe spaces for women in these seasons?

Scripture for Meditation

- *"He gives strength to the weary and increases the power of the weak." - Isaiah 40:29.*
- *"You are fearfully and wonderfully made." - Psalm 139:14.*
- *"To everything there is a season." - Ecclesiastes 3:1.*
- *"Carry each other's burdens, and in this way you will fulfil the law of Christ." - Galatians 6:2.*
- *"Your bodies are temples of the Holy Spirit." - 1 Corinthians 6:19.*

CHAPTER THREE

Unseen Illnesses: Endometriosis, PCOS, Fibroids and Fibromyalgia

> ❝
> Carry each other's burdens, and in this way you will fulfil the law of Christ.
> – GALATIANS 6:2
> ❞

Invisible conditions drain energy, fertility and confidence while often being dismissed as "exaggeration." This chapter names these illnesses, validates women's pain and reclaims dignity for bodies under strain.

1. The Hidden Reality

In the quiet of the counselling room, I have often been the first person to believe a woman's story of pain. She had already been dismissed by doctors, doubted by family or told that it was all in her head. Many live with chronic conditions that are not visible but cut deeply into their physical, emotional, and spiritual wellbeing.

Endometriosis, fibromyalgia, polycystic ovary syndrome (PCOS) and uterine fibroids are among the most common. They drain energy, disrupt fertility, damage relationships and erode confidence but the physical, emotional and spiritual impact is still minimised or ignored.

2. Conditions That Go Unseen

- **Endometriosis** involves tissue similar to the uterine lining growing outside the womb. It causes pain, heavy bleeding, infertility and exhaustion.
- **Fibromyalgia** brings widespread pain, fatigue, difficulties with memory and focus often called "fibro fog."
- **PCOS** is a hormonal disorder that affects weight, fertility and emotional stability.
- **Fibroids** are non-cancerous growths of the uterus that can lead to heavy bleeding, anaemia, and complications in pregnancy.

These conditions reach far beyond the body. They affect how a woman sees herself, relates to loved ones and also how she approaches her faith.

3. The Pain of Disbelief

Again and again women speak of not being believed. A woman writhing in pain is told she is exaggerating. Another is told that heavy bleeding is "normal", some are told they are overreacting, imagining symptoms or being "too emotional." Years can pass before a proper diagnosis is made.

This disbelief does more than delay treatment. It plants doubt. A woman begins to question her own perception of pain, value, and also her identity as God's beloved. Scripture warns us: *"To answer before listening is folly and shame" (Proverbs 18:13).* Listening is not only good practice but it is an act of compassion.

4. Isolation and Hidden Grief

Chronic conditions often push women into isolation. Friends and colleagues grow impatient when she cancels plans. Employers see absence rather than perseverance. Even within churches, support may shrink to a quick prayer rather than sustained care.

The Psalmist wrote: *"The Lord is close to the broken-hearted and saves those who are crushed in spirit" (Psalm 34:18).* Yet many women feel far from the community, as if their pain makes them an inconvenience. Their grief is doubled: the pain itself and the loneliness that follows.

5. A Counselling Response

Christian counselling can become a lifeline in this wilderness. It begins with three simple but transformative commitments:
- **Believe her story.** To be believed is often the first taste of healing.
- **Honour the body.** Encourage women to rebuild trust with their own bodies. Scripture calls the body *"a temple of the Holy Spirit" (1 Corinthians 6:19–20)*. Even in pain, it is sacred.
- **Empower with tools and theology.** Equip women with strategies for self-care and advocacy while reminding them that suffering does not diminish their worth before God.

Closing Thought

Invisible illnesses reshape daily life and to suffer is heavy but to suffer without being believed is crushing. Women with chronic conditions are not weak or exaggerating. They are carrying burdens that deserve recognition and compassion.

Isaiah wrote: *"If you spend yourselves on behalf of the hungry and satisfy the needs of the oppressed, then your light will rise in the darkness" (Isaiah 58:10)*. When we acknowledge and stand with women in their suffering, we reflect the light of Christ. *"Carry each other's burdens." (Galatians 6:2)*.

Reflection & Discussion

1. Have I ever doubted my own pain because others dismissed it?
2. How have hidden conditions shaped my relationship with God, my family, or myself?
3. What might it mean to be truly believed and supported?
4. How can my church or community walk alongside women living with chronic pain?

Scripture for Meditation

- "The Lord is close to the broken-hearted and saves those who are crushed in spirit." - Psalm 34:18.
- "Your body is a temple of the Holy Spirit, honour God with your bodies." - 1 Corinthians 6:19–20.
- "He heals the broken-hearted and binds up their wounds." - Psalm 147:3.
- "To answer before listening is folly and shame." - Proverbs 18:13.
- "He gives strength to the weary." - Isaiah 40:29.

CHAPTER FOUR

The Quiet Mind: Anxiety, Depression, ADHD and Postnatal struggles

> **❝**
> *Cast all your anxiety on Him because He cares for you.*
> – 1 PETER 5:7
> **❞**

Behind polished smiles, many women wrestle with fragile mental health. This chapter uncovers the hidden cost of anxiety, depression, and overlooked conditions, affirming that God meets us even in fractured thoughts.

1. Mental Health Hidden Behind Smiles

Many women carry anxiety, depression or exhaustion behind a polished smile. In the workplace they perform with excellence. In church they serve faithfully. In the family they hold everything together. Yet in private they collapse under the weight of mental distress.

I have met women who after greeting me cheerfully and are safely behind closed doors, they release the mask and confess that they have not slept in weeks. Others whisper of despair while appearing to thrive publicly. Their pain is invisible, yet it is real.

2. Conditions Often Overlooked

- **Postnatal depression** is often reduced to "baby blues." Mothers hesitate to speak whilst fearing judgement or being labelled ungratefully.
- **Anxiety disorders** can be masked by achievement. The more capable a woman appears, the more likely her distress is missed.
- **ADHD in women** is rarely recognised. Symptoms such as emotional dysregulation, forgetfulness and burn-out are mistaken for character flaws or mood problems.

When mental health struggles are unnamed, women feel even more isolated.

3. Gender Bias in Care

Medical and psychological systems have often misread women's mental health. Distress is brushed aside as hormonal, exaggerated or simply part of being female. Girls with ADHD are overlooked because they are not disruptive in school.

Women in their thirties or forties are told their anxiety is "just stress."

Galatians 3:28 reminds us, *"There is neither male nor female, for you are all one in Christ Jesus."* In God's eyes, women's experiences are not secondary. Yet too often, their pain is minimised in systems meant to heal.

4. Cultural Expectations of Strength

In many African and diaspora communities, strength is seen as survival. Women are taught to endure without complaint. Tears are suppressed, sadness is hidden. Silence becomes a badge of honour.

Yet scripture says there is *"a time to weep and a time to laugh, a time to mourn and a time to dance" (Ecclesiastes 3:4).* Denying sorrow does not make us holy. It makes us human. Lament is prayer in its rawest form.

5. The Counsellor's Role

When women bring these hidden struggles into the counselling room, the task is to create a safe space where masks are not needed. That work includes:
- **Building trust.** Giving permission to be vulnerable without fear of judgement.

- **Confronting shame.** Many carry guilt for needing help therefore reminding them that God does not condemn their humanity is paramount
- **Equipping for advocacy.** Supporting women in describing their struggles clearly to health professionals, workplaces, or families.
- **Integrating theology.** Emphasising a God who sees, comforts, and redeems. He does not demand performance but welcomes honesty.

Closing Thought

Mental health struggles often hide behind success, service, or spirituality. But the God who formed us does not overlook what is unseen. He is gentle with the fragile and close to the weary.

Isaiah wrote of Christ: *"A bruised reed He will not break, and a smouldering wick He will not snuff" (Isaiah 42:3).* Women who feel like smouldering wicks must know that God will never extinguish them. He tends, restores and strengthens.

Reflection & Discussion

1. Have I felt pressure to keep smiling when my mental health was breaking?
2. What messages from culture, family, or church have shaped how I handle weakness?

3. How can my community become safer for women struggling silently?
4. Where do I see God's presence when my mind feels heavy?

Scripture for Meditation

- "The Lord is close to the broken-hearted and saves those who are crushed in spirit." - Psalm 34:18.
- "Come to Me, all you who are weary and burdened, and I will give you rest."
- - Matthew 11:28.
- "A bruised reed He will not break, and a smouldering wick He will not snuff out." - Isaiah 42:3.

PART TWO:
Silence in Relationships and Systems

Here we expose how silence thrives in homes, churches and workplaces. From abuse behind closed doors to distorted teachings, hidden emotional labour, discrimination, shame and trauma. This part reveals how unhealthy systems deepen women's pain.

CHAPTER FIVE

Behind Closed Doors: Abuse in Christian homes

> ❝
> Have nothing to do with the fruitless deeds of darkness but rather expose them.
> – EPHESIANS 5:11
> ❞

The home is meant to nurture, yet too often it conceals abuse under a cloak of faith. This chapter confronts the painful paradox of violence hidden within Christian households.

1. The Painful Paradox

The home should be a place of safety and for Christian families, it is meant to reflect the character of Christ. Most especially, love, gentleness, and truth. However, behind closed doors abuse in Christian households is a hidden crisis. Emotional, physical, verbal, sexual and spiritual abuse can occur even where the Bible is quoted also when prayers are offered. Often, the abuse is concealed beneath a veneer of respectability reinforced by silence, misused Scripture, or distorted theology. *"Have nothing to do with the fruitless deeds of darkness but rather expose them." - Ephesians 5:11.*

Many suffer silently, trapped by distorted theology or religious obligation.I have counselled women who prayed faithfully, led Bible studies and served in ministry while silently enduring verbal cruelty, physical harm, or coercion in the name of scripture. The very place designed for nurture became a prison.

2. The Many Faces of Abuse

Abuse wears many masks in Christian homes:
- **Emotional abuse:** manipulation, criticism, shaming, and withholding affection.
- Physical abuse: violence or threats of harm.
- **Verbal abuse:** insults, intimidation or degrading language.
- **Sexual abuse:** unwanted or coerced sexual activity even within marriage.
- **Financial and dowry abuse:** women pressured under cultural obligations such as high bride price with threats of repayment or rejection.
- **Spiritual abuse:** scripture or religious authority twisted to control and silence.

The damage is not only physical or emotional but deeply spiritual. A woman may begin to question God's goodness because His word has been misused against her, or they feel like they are betraying God by speaking up to protect themselves.

3. The Misuse of Scripture

Some of the deepest wounds come when scripture is weaponised, so verses meant to teach love and humility are twisted into tools of control.
- *"Wives, submit to your husbands" (Ephesians 5:22)* quoted without the next verse: *"Husbands, love your wives as Christ loved the church" (v.25)*.

Forgiveness demanded without repentance or accountability.

- *"Children obey your parents"* used to excuse cruelty in the home *(Ephesians 6:1-3)*, without being taught that abuse is never God's will.
- *"Women should remain silent" (1 Corinthians 14:34)* removed from its cultural setting and misapplied to suppress women in church and family life.

This twisting of God's word distorts His heart because he never condones oppression but rather he is a God of justice and compassion.

4. Silence in the Church

Abuse thrives in silence therefore many survivors are told to "pray harder," "stay for the sake of the marriage," or "keep the family's reputation." Sadly, in some churches, image is protected above the safety of the vulnerable.When there is no safe space for honest conversation, vulnerability is replaced by performance, and the wounds continue to deepen behind closed doors

There are moments when silence can serve prayer or reflection. But when silence is enforced by a stubborn spouse to cover violence or sin, communication is deliberately withdrawn as a tool of punishment which becomes destructive. The church must not confuse patience with complicity.

5. God's Heart for the Oppressed

Scripture is clear about God's response to injustice:
- *"The Lord is a refuge for the oppressed, a stronghold in times of trouble" (Psalm 9:9).*
- *"Rescue the weak and needy; deliver them from the hand of the wicked" (Psalm 82:4).*
- *Jesus proclaimed He came "to bind up the broken-hearted, to proclaim freedom for the captives" (Isaiah 61:1).*

God does not ask His daughters to remain in danger but rather his heart is for protection, not destruction.

6. Pathways Toward Healing

Breaking free begins with the truth. Naming abuse is the first step toward healing as it acknowledges the reality that abuse is not just a "marital problem" or a "discipline issue" but a sin. For some women, this means confiding in a counsellor or trusted friend whilst for others, it involves seeking pastoral and legal support to secure safety.

Counselling creates space to:
- Affirm that abuse is never God's will.
- Provide emotional care and spiritual reassurance.
- Support practical steps toward safety and recovery.

Healing takes time but God is present in the journey. He lifts shame, restores dignity and gives courage to rebuild.

Closing Thought

Abuse in a Christian home is a deep betrayal. It wounds the body, spirit, and faith. Yet the silence that protects it must be broken, God is not honoured by secrecy that shelters sin. He is glorified when truth is spoken and the oppressed are set free.

In Christ there is hope for safety, justice and peace.

Reflection & Discussion

1. How has scripture been used in ways that silence or control women in families or churches?
2. What barriers make it difficult for survivors to speak out?
3. How can faith communities become safe places for truth and healing?
4. Which scriptures remind me of God's care for the oppressed?

Scripture for Meditation

- *"The Lord is a refuge for the oppressed, a stronghold in times of trouble." - Psalm 9:9.*
- *"Rescue the weak and needy; deliver them from the hand of the wicked." - Psalm 82:4*
- *"Have nothing to do with the fruitless deeds of darkness, but rather expose them."*
- *- Ephesians 5:11.*
- *"He heals the broken-hearted and binds up their wounds." - Psalm 147:3.*

CHAPTER SIX

Twisted Teachings: When submission becomes suppression

> *Wives, submit yourselves to your own husbands as you do to the Lord.*
> – EPHESIANS 5:22

Submission in scripture was meant to reflect mutual love, not control. Here we examine how distorted theology robs women of voice and identity and what true partnership should look like.

1. The Burden of Misapplied Submission

Submission is an action of accepting a superior force or to the will or authority of another person. In the Bible however, submission is meant to reflect humility, respect and trust before God. It is a posture of love within a marriage not an excuse for control but many women are taught a distorted version that leaves them voiceless, fearful and in spiritual bondage.

I have sat with wives who longed to honour God but felt suffocated in relationships where their words carried no weight. They were told that to question their husbands was disobedience even when their needs were ignored. Submission, instead of being mutual and life- giving became heavy and silencing.

2. When Strength Turns to Silence

In Christian communities, submission is sometimes taught as a hierarchy where men lead and women follow without question. When this teaching is misused, women lose their voice and sense of identity.

In the counselling room, I have encountered many women who feel spiritually trapped, unable to reconcile their emotional well- being with their understanding of biblical submission. One woman shared in a session:

"I am told to honour my husband but my heart is so heavy with resentment. I feel as though my voice is never heard. I know I am supposed to submit but I don't know how to submit to someone who doesn't listen to me."

Her words echo the silent cry of many whose sincere desire to honour God through biblical submission is clouded by emotional pain and relational dysfunction.

Her admission-" I am told to honour my husband, but my heart is so heavy with resentment-reveals the inner conflict between her faith and her emotional reality.

Many internalise blame. If a marriage is struggling they believe it is because they have not "submitted properly." Some stop recognising themselves beyond the roles of a wife and a mother. Dreams, opinions and even faith are swallowed by the expectation of quiet compliance.

One woman told me, "I am told to honour my husband, but my heart feels heavy with resentment." I want to submit but I don't know how to submit to someone who never hears me. Her cry echoed the struggle of many who equate faithfulness with silence.

3. The Emotional Toll

The misuse of submission can leave deep scars:
- **Loss of voice.** Women feel their perspectives are irrelevant.
- **Fear.** Disagreement may be met with anger, withdrawal of love and affection, or undue punishment.
- **Diminished worth.** Identity becomes tied to serving without ever being seen.

These experiences are not God's design. They are the fruit of distorted teaching and unhealthy power dynamics.

4. The True Picture of Submission

Ephesians 5:21 calls believers to *"submit to one another out of reverence for Christ."* Mutual submission means each partner serves the other in love. Husbands are instructed to love their wives as Christ loved the church with sacrifice, tenderness, and care.

Biblical submission is never about erasing a woman's voice. It is about partnership. A healthy marriage thrives when both are respected and valued as equal heirs of God's grace *(1 Peter 3:7)*.

5. When Submission Becomes Abuse

Submission can be weaponised in abusive relationships. A husband may demand obedience while ignoring his call to sacrificial love. Gaslighting, withholding affection, and manipulation can all be masked as "headship." This is not submission but called control.

God does not condone abuse and no verse of scripture justifies harm. Where women are silenced by distorted teaching, the church must speak the truth. More to that, submission does not mean enduring fear or oppression.

6. Counselling Pathways

In counselling, women caught in unhealthy submission dynamics need to rediscover their worth and voice. Helpful approaches include:
- **Challenging false beliefs.** Replacing thoughts like, "If I speak up, I dishonour God," with truth. "God values my voice and dignity."
- **Reframing identity.** Narrating and reinforcing trauma-informed approaches which help women see themselves as whole persons not silent servants.
- **Encouraging safe boundaries.** Healthy submission does not mean tolerating harm.

Counselling also invites men to see leadership not as power but as service. A marriage rooted in love and respect reflects Christ far more than one built on fear.

7. The Church's Responsibility

Churches must teach submission as mutual not one-sided. Leaders should therefore;
- Preach the full context of scripture.
- Address distorted power dynamics openly.
- Provide safe spaces where women can speak freely about struggles.

The example of Abigail in *1 Samuel 25* shows wise submission. She honoured her household by protecting it from her husband's reckless choices. She did not passively enable her husband's reckless behaviour and acted with discernment, and courage, aligning herself with God's justice.

Closing Thought

Submission when rightly understood is not bondage but love expressed through humility and respect. It does not silence a woman's voice or erase her worth. True submission flows both ways by reflecting the relationship between Christ and His church, love that protects, serves and honours.

Let us build marriages where women are not silenced but cherished and where their voices contribute to flourishing homes rooted in grace.

Reflection & Discussion

1. Have I seen a scripture used to silence or control? How did it shape my understanding of God?
2. Where have I confused submission with suppression in my own life or community?
3. What practical steps could make marriages reflect mutual respect and partnership?
4. How can the church protect women from distorted teaching about submission?

Scripture for Meditation

- "Husbands, love your wives, just as Christ loved the church and gave Himself up for her." - Ephesians 5:25.
- "Submit to one another out of reverence for Christ." - Ephesians 5:21.
- "Perfect love drives out fear." (1 John 4:18)
- "The Lord is a refuge for the oppressed, a stronghold in times of trouble." -Psalm 9:9.

CHAPTER SEVEN

The Invisible Load: Emotional labour and unshared responsibility

> ❝
> *Cast all your anxiety on Him because He cares for you.*
> *- 1 PETER 5:7*
> ❞

Managing relationships, soothing tensions, and anticipating needs often falls silently on women. This chapter exposes the cost of carrying unseen burdens without recognition or rest.

1. The Hidden Weight of Unseen Work

Many women carry responsibilities that are invisible yet relentless. They manage tasks and emotions thereby soothing tensions, anticipating needs, remembering details, and keeping peace. This hidden labour drains energy and self-worth even as it appears noble to others.

Unlike physical work, this type of burden is spiritual, psychological and relational in nature. The emotional labour is hard to measure. It leaves no clock-in or clock-out yet it consumes a woman's day and mind. In the counselling room, I often hear women describe themselves as weary to the bone though no one around them seems to notice.

2. Emotional Labour Defined

Emotional labour is the constant effort to manage relationships. It is the remembering of birthdays, quiet keeping of family harmony, planning of meals, anticipation of conflict, and the soothing of others' frustrations.

This role often falls to women by default in homes, workplaces and even churches. It may look like care but when unshared it becomes exploitation. It asks women to empty themselves continually without acknowledgement or rest.

Colossians 3:23 reminds us, *"Whatever you do, work at it with all your heart, as working for the Lord."* This verse, so often quoted, is not a call to endless depletion. God's design includes joy and balance but not exhaustion disguised as holiness.

3. Caregiving Without Recognition

Women are often expected to provide care not only to children but also to ageing parents, sick relatives, and entire communities. While this care is essential, it is frequently unpaid, unacknowledged and assumed. Over time, it becomes an invisible thread that ties women to unending duty while others move freely.

Faith communities can unintentionally deepen this expectation. Calls to sacrificial service may leave women believing that asking for help is selfish or ungodly. Yet *Isaiah 40:29 says, "He gives strength to the weary and increases the power of the weak."* God invites us to admit our limits, not conceal them.

4. The Myth of Doing It All

Modern culture praises the woman who appears to balance the identity of mother, minister, professional, homemaker and friend- all while staying cheerful, beautiful and devout. This myth is destructive because it sets women up for guilt, shame and burnout.

Even Jesus stepped away from crowds to rest and pray *(Luke 5:16)*. If the Son of God modelled boundaries, then rest is not indulgence but obedience. Women are not called to carry every burden alone.

5. Counselling Pathways

When women share the weight of invisible labour the first step is to validate what they carry. Often, naming the unseen brings relief and Counselling also helps to:
- **Challenge unhealthy beliefs.** Value is not measured by productivity.
- **Restore boundaries.** Rest and margin are sacred, not optional.
- **Encourage shared responsibility.** Families, churches, and workplaces must learn to share the load fairly.
- **Reframe service.** Serving others should flow from love, not compulsion or fear of failing expectations.

Closing Thought

The invisible load is not a sign of weakness but of hidden strength. Yet God never intended women to live under unending strain. When we name these labours, share them, and set boundaries, freedom begins. True discipleship is not endless doing but resting in the grace of Christ.

Reflection & Discussion

1. What hidden responsibilities do I carry that others rarely see?
2. How have cultural or church expectations shaped my view of rest and service?

3. What conversations could help redistribute burdens in my home, workplace, or ministry?
4. Where might God be inviting me to lay down what I was never meant to carry alone?

Scripture for Meditation

- *"Come to Me, all you who are weary and burdened, and I will give you rest." - Matthew 11:28.*
- *"He makes me lie down in green pastures, He leads me beside quiet waters, He refreshes my soul." - Psalm 23:1-3.*
- *"Be still, and know that I am God." - Psalm 46:10.*
- *"In quietness and trust is your strength." (Isaiah 30:15)*

CHAPTER EIGHT

Workplace Wounds: Microaggressions, motherhood penalty, discrimination

> *Speak up for those who cannot speak for themselves, for the rights of all who are destitute.*
> – PROVERBS 31:8

Many women enter workplaces full of talent yet encounter daily slights, stalled promotions, or unspoken exclusion. This chapter sheds light on subtle but corrosive injustices at work.

1. Workplaces as Battlegrounds

The workplace is meant to be a space where people grow, use their gifts, and build dignity through contribution. For many women, however, it is marked by subtle wounds being overlooked, dismissed or judged more harshly than male colleagues.

I have spoken with women who carry a quiet dread each morning. Not because of the work itself, but because of the constant need to prove their worth in environments that undervalue them.

2. Microaggressions

Microaggressions are small, often unthinking remarks or behaviours that reveal bias. They may seem insignificant in isolation but accumulate into heavy burdens.

A woman's ideas may be ignored until repeated by a man. Her accent may be mocked in passing. Her competence may be questioned in ways her male peers never face. She is interrupted, excluded or patronised.

These daily slights leave scars, they communicate that she does not belong even when she is fully qualified and capable. Over time, confidence is eroded not through one event but through a steady drip of dismissal.

3. The Motherhood Penalty

For working mothers, the bias deepens. A woman returning from maternity leave may find her commitment questioned. She is passed over for promotions or excluded from key projects. Meanwhile, men who become fathers are often seen as more stable and dedicated.

This disparity known as the 'motherhood penalty' is widespread. Women speak of feeling torn and accused of neglecting children if they pursue work or seen as less ambitious if they prioritise family. The judgement is unspoken but ever-present.

As believers, we must challenge these assumptions. Scripture honours both work and family. *Proverbs 31* describes a woman whose household thrives and whose business dealings are respected. Her worth is not diminished by her roles but celebrated in their fullness.

4. Unspoken Discrimination

Some wounds in the workplace are less visible but just as damaging. These include unwritten rules, unaddressed behaviours, or cultures that disadvantage women without ever being named. Examples include:
- Exclusion from informal networks: Decisions and opportunities are often shaped in after- hours settings where women, especially mothers or carers are absent
- Unrealistic expectations of availability: Work cultures may reward constant presence or late-night responsiveness- standards incompatible with responsibilities.
- Neglect of health-related needs: Lack of consideration for women's health issues (such as menstruation, menopause, or maternity care) can subtly undermine their participation and advancement.

These realities are rarely addressed openly which makes them harder to confront and can be as damaging as explicit bias. They communicate whose presence and wellbeing truly matters, while forcing women to adapt quietly, doubting whether their experience is valid. Yet silence protects only the systems that perpetuate inequality.

5. A Counselling and Pastoral Response

When women bring workplace wounds into counselling, the task is not only to support their resilience but to affirm their right to dignity. Healing involves:
- **Naming experiences honestly.** Giving language to subtle injustices which breaks the power of confusion.
- **Rebuilding confidence.** Helping women reclaim their worth beyond biased judgments.
- **Encouraging advocacy.** Equipping women to raise concerns constructively in workplaces or seek legal and organisational support where needed.
- **Grounding identity in Christ.** Reminding them that their value is not determined by human systems but by God who calls them worthy and beloved.

Closing Thought

Workplace wounds are often unseen by those in power but they shape lives profoundly. Women bear the cost of daily microaggressions, motherhood penalty, and the ache of being overlooked.

Yet God's word affirms dignity, He calls His daughters capable, wise and full of value. As a community of faith, we must not only comfort those wounded but also speak truth into systems that diminish them. Advocacy is therefore part of discipleship.

Reflection & Discussion

1. Have I experienced or witnessed subtle discrimination in the workplace? How did it affect me?
2. How as motherhood or assumptions about it shaped opportunities for the women I know?
3. What steps could churches or faith communities take to affirm and support working women?
4. Where might God be calling me to speak up for justice in professional spaces?

Scripture for Meditation

- *"Speak up for those who cannot speak for themselves." – Proverbs 31:8.*
- *"The labourer deserves his wages." – 1 Timothy 5:18.*
- *"Let justice roll on like a river, righteousness like a never-failing stream." – Amos 5:24.*

CHAPTER NINE

The Shadow of Shame:
Cultural and spiritual weight of secrecy

> ❝
> *Those who look to Him are radiant;*
> *their faces are never covered with shame.*
> – PSALM 34:5
> ❞

Shame whispers that women are unworthy—whether from past mistakes, cultural stigma, or church judgement. This chapter explores how shame takes root and how Christ restores dignity.

1. The Heavy Shadow of Shame

Shame is one of the most powerful silencers in a woman's life. It does not always come with words but it lingers in the unspoken, sideway glances, whispered gossip and the weight of what cannot be said.

I have sat with women who live under the shadow of past mistakes, broken relationships, abortions, miscarriages or choices made in desperation. Others carry shame for what was done to them. Although they were the victims, shame convinces them that they are unworthy of love, forgiveness and even of God's care.

2. How Shame Takes Root

Shame thrives where honesty is not allowed. In many Christian families, a daughter who becomes pregnant outside of marriage is cast out while the man who fathered the child faces little consequences. In churches, women who have divorced or struggled with infertility often feel they have failed spiritually.

Some women are told their bodies are sources of temptation and that their value depends on purity or obedience. When life takes another course they carry the silent message: "You are less. You are defiled. You are not enough."

These lies wound deeply. They trap women in secrecy and distance them from the very community that should offer grace.

3. Shame and the Gospel

The Gospel speaks the opposite. Jesus met women in their places of deepest shame and restored their dignity publicly.

- To the woman caught in adultery, He said, *"Neither do I condemn you" (John 8:11)*.
- To the woman with the issue of blood, He called her *"Daughter"* in front of the crowd *(Luke 8:48)*.
- To the Samaritan woman at the well, He revealed His identity and entrusted her with His message *(John 4:26–29)*.

Christ did not turn away from women marked by shame. He honoured them, spoke life to them and gave them back their voices.

4. The Cost of Carrying Shame

Shame silences prayer. A woman convinced that God is disappointed may stop approaching Him altogether. It damages relationships as she withdraws for fear of exposure. It weighs on the body through anxiety, depression and illness.

Left unspoken, shame becomes a prison. It shapes identity until a woman no longer sees herself as God's daughter but only through the lens of failure.

5. A Path Toward Freedom

Healing from shame is not quick but it is possible. In counselling and pastoral care steps include:
- **Naming the source.** Bringing hidden pain into the light weakens shame's grip.

- **Reframing identity.** Reminding women that their worth rests not in past choices or others' opinions but in being image-bearers of God.
- **Embracing grace.** The cross of Christ declares forgiveness completely. Nothing is beyond His redemption.
- **Building a safe community.** Healing requires spaces where women are heard without judgement and welcomed as a whole.

Closing Thought

Shame is a heavy cloak but God never intended His daughters to wear it. The blood of Christ does not only forgive sin but it restores dignity. Those who look to Him are radiant not because of their perfection but because His love covers them.

No woman is defined by her past. In Christ, she is free.

Reflection & Discussion

1. What silent shame do I carry that I have never voiced?
2. How has family, culture or church shaped my sense of worth?
3. Where do I need to hear again the words of Jesus: *"Neither do I condemn you"*?
4. How can my community create spaces that lift shame rather than deepen it?

Scripture for Meditation

- *"Those who look to Him are radiant; their faces are never covered with shame." – Psalm 34:5.*
- *"There is now no condemnation for those who are in Christ Jesus." – Romans 8:1.*
- *"Daughter, your faith has healed you. Go in peace." – Luke 8:48.*

CHAPTER TEN

Bodies Under Scrutiny – Infertility, miscarriage, abortion and judgement

> *Children are a heritage from the Lord,*
> *offspring a reward from Him.*
> – PSALM 127:3

Reproductive choices and struggles are deeply personal yet often judged harshly. Here we look at how women's bodies become battlegrounds for culture and church, and how compassion can replace condemnation.

1. The Unspoken Battles

Few areas of a woman's life invite more scrutiny than her choices about reproduction. Decisions about contraception, childbearing, infertility or abortion are often met with judgement, silence or control. These are intimate matters of the body and soul, yet many women are denied the dignity of making decisions without pressure or fear.

In counselling, I have heard stories of women shamed for not having children soon after marriage, criticised for having too many or questioned for choosing not to have any. Others describe pressure from family or culture to continue dangerous pregnancies or to prioritise fertility over health. Each story reveals how reproductive autonomy is often eroded quietly hence leaving women burdened with guilt.

2. Cultural and Community Expectations

In many cultures, a woman's worth is tied to her ability to bear children. In African settings, infertility can invite ridicule or rejection from in-laws. In some Christian communities, contraception is judged as a lack of faith. Women who face miscarriage or stillbirth are whispered about as though their grief is somehow their fault.

These expectations leave women feeling trapped between honouring their faith, meeting cultural demands and caring for their own wellbeing.

3. Infertility and the Weight of Silence

Infertility is more common than many realise, yet it remains shrouded in silence. Couples walk through years of disappointment while fielding endless questions: *"When will you have children?"*

For women, the pain can be compounded by stigma. The Bible records the anguish of Sarah, Rachel, and Hannah. Their cries remind us that the ache of barrenness is not new. What is tragic is how often modern communities still fail to offer compassion, leaving women to bear sorrow alone.

4. Abortion and Hidden Grief

Abortion remains one of the most silenced subjects in Christian spaces. Women who have walked this road often do so in secrecy, fearing judgement from their community. Some carry regret, others relief mixed with grief, and so forth. Whatever the circumstances, silence leaves wounds unhealed.

Martha sat in my office with her hands clenched tightly on her lap. Her posture was poised elegant even, but her eyes betrayed her. They darted around the room, searching for a safe place to rest. But shame rarely gives the soul rest.

"I haven't told anyone,"She whispered."Not even my husband. I carry it alone."

Her story wasn't uncommon. A past mistake. A choice made in desperation. A secret buried under years of trying to "be better." Martha a woman of faith, known in her church for her kindness and hospitality. But hidden behind her Sunday smile was a painful truth- she had undergone an abortion in her early twenties, long before her salvation. Now, decades later, despite receiving Christ's forgiveness, she continues to punish herself for past sins- shame still follows her like a shadow.

In my counselling room, Martha; in addition to her emotional burden, carried physical and psychological struggles from the medical procedure, it was layered upon her Christian faith and devotional to pastoral work. Every time she made a mistake, be it small or significant, she would spiral into a cycle of self-condemnation. "I always feel like I'm dirty," she confessed. "No matter how much I pray."

Her internal belief was this: "I am unworthy!'

A prisoner to a past- this is the insidious nature of shame. Unlike guilt, which says, "I've done something wrong," shame declares, "There is something wrong with me."

Christ's posture toward women was never condemnation but restoration. *John 8* records Him saying, *"Neither do I condemn you. Go and sin no more."* This does not erase accountability, but it does remind us that grace is always greater than shame.

The Bible gives us a powerful image of shame and redemption in *John 8*. A woman caught in the very act of adultery was dragged before Jesus. Her accusers, armed with stones and self-righteous indignation, demanded judgment.

But Jesus stoops down and writes in the dust He then stands and says, *"Let any one of you who is without sin be the first to throw a stone."* (John 8:7)

One by one, the stones fall, the crowd disperses. And there she stands, vulnerable, humiliated and likely trembling in fear.

Yet Jesus looks her in the eyes and says, *"Neither do I condemn you."* (John 8:11)

This is the voice every shame- bound woman needs to hear. Not the voice of accusation but of grace. Not condemnation, but compassion.

5. The Church's Response

Churches often struggle to hold these issues with truth and compassion together. Some lean toward silence and others toward condemnation. Both responses wound. However, what is required is a pastoral voice that speaks of life as a gift whilst offering mercy to those facing complex realities.

Practical ways forward include:
- Teaching about reproductive health without fear or stigma.
- Supporting couples facing infertility with prayer, presence and practical help.
- Creating safe spaces for women who have experienced miscarriages, stillbirth or abortions to grieve and heal.
- Affirming that women's choices and bodies are not public property but belong to God who cares deeply for them.

- Reframing identity by replacing lies ("I am unworthy") with God's truth *("I am fearfully and wonderfully made" - Psalm 139: 14)*.
- Engaging Scripture and meditating on passages that affirm forgiveness and restoration.

6. Counselling Pathways

When women bring these struggles to counselling, the role is to:
- **Validate their story.** Every journey is unique.
- **Address internalised shame.** Replace the belief "I am less" with "I am loved."
- **Provide space for grief.** Allow tears for what was lost, whether children, pregnancies or dreams.
- **Integrate faith with compassion.** Point to a God who values life but never abandons women in their struggle.

Closing Thought

Reproductive choices and struggles are among the most intimate parts of a woman's life yet they are often met with the harshest judgement. God's word honours life and children yet His heart also overflows with mercy for His daughters.

To walk with women in these silent battles is to reflect Christ Himself: full of grace and truth.

Reflection & Discussion

1. How has culture, family, or church shaped my view of womanhood and childbearing?
2. Where have I felt judged or silenced in reproductive decisions?
3. How can faith communities support women walking through infertility, miscarriage or abortion without shame?
4. What scriptures remind me of God's mercy in times of grief and struggle?

Scripture for Meditation

- *"Children are a heritage from the Lord, offspring a reward from Him." - Psalm 127:3.*
- *"He settles the childless woman in her home as a happy mother of children." - Psalm 113:9.*
- *"Neither do I condemn you. Go now and leave your life of sin." - John 8:11.*
- *"The Lord is close to the broken-hearted and saves those who are crushed in spirit." - Psalm 34:18.*

CHAPTER ELEVEN

Trauma That Lingers:
Violence, coercion, and cultural silencing

> ❝
> The Lord is a refuge for the oppressed,
> a stronghold in times of trouble.
> – PSALM 9:9
> ❞

Violence leaves scars on body, mind, and spirit. This chapter confronts trauma's enduring impact, from domestic abuse to forced marriage, and the silence that imprisons survivors.

1. The Lasting Impact of Violence

Violence leaves marks that go far deeper than bruises. Long after wounds on the body have healed, memories remain replayed in the mind, carried in the nervous system and stored in the heart.

Women who survive violence often struggle with fear, shame and the constant effort to appear strong. Some bury their experiences believing silence will protect them since choosing freedom often entails high costs: family estrangement, community rejection, or loss of support networks. Women may face spiritual confusion and loneliness amid these sacrifices. For some who do share, they are sometimes met with disbelief, blame, or minimisation.

The silence that follows violence can wound as deeply as the violence itself.

2. Trauma in Women's Lives

Trauma is not only what happens but how it lingers. For women, it often arises from:
- **Domestic violence** that erodes safety in their own homes.
- **Sexual assault** that strips dignity and leaves lasting scars.
- **Childhood abuse** that shapes self-worth and trust into adulthood.
- **War, displacement or forced migration** that uproot identity and belonging.

Trauma can lead to nightmares, flashbacks, anxiety, depression and difficulties in relationships. It is not a weakness but the body's response to overwhelming harm.

Cultural Realities in Africa

In many African settings, trauma is compounded by cultural practices. Girls may be forced into marriage at a very young age by close family members in exchange for material gain. These child marriages often lock women into lives of vulnerability, where their voices are silenced and their complaints dismissed as "bad manners."

In Uganda, for example, there have been instances where spiritual language is misused to legitimise coercion. Men have said, *"Yesu akuntumye"*- translated, *"Jesus has sent me to marry you",* as a way of cloaking harmful intentions with false piety. In other cases, respected church members have used faith and tradition as tools of intimidation, excusing mistreatment under the guise of religious duty.

Such distortions of culture and faith not only wound women but also corrode the sacredness of marriage itself. For survivors, the trauma is personal *and* systemic, embedded in structures of silence, power and misuse of Scripture.

3. Why Women Remain Silent

Many women keep their trauma hidden. They fear being blamed: *"What were you wearing?" "Why didn't you leave?"* In some cultures, family honour outweighs a woman's safety pressuring her into silence.

Within faith communities, silence is sometimes reinforced by appeals to forgiveness without accountability or by misplaced concern for an abuser's reputation. Women are urged to endure rather than to seek safety.

This culture of silence allows trauma to fester instead of healing.

Further, language barriers further marginalise women, limiting access to healthcare, counselling, and legal protection. Systemic neglect often compounds these barriers, leaving women without adequate resources or advocacy.

Christian counsellors must be sensitive to these challenges, seeking culturally informed approaches and interpreter services to ensure voices are heard and needs met.

4. God's Heart for Survivors

The Bible reveals God's compassion for the oppressed. He defends the vulnerable, lifts the broken-hearted and brings justice to the mistreated.
- *"He heals the broken-hearted and binds up their wounds" (Psalm 147:3).*
- *"Rescue the weak and needy, deliver them from the hand of the wicked" (Psalm 82:4).*
- Jesus restored dignity to women who had been shunned by giving them back their voices and honour.

God does not turn away from survivors of violence but He stands with them.

5. The Path of Healing

Healing from trauma is slow and layered. Counselling provides a safe place to rebuild safety and trust. Some helpful steps include:
- Restoring safety. Survivors must first know they are secure whether physically, emotionally, or spiritually.
- Processing memories. Trauma-informed therapy helps women face painful memories at a pace they can bear.
- Reframing identity. Trauma whispers, "You are damaged." God declares, "You are my beloved daughter."
- Encouraging lament and prayer. Survivors can bring even raw painful emotions before God.

Healing does not erase the past but allows women to live beyond it.

6. The Role of the Church

Churches must become sanctuaries where survivors are believed, protected and supported. This means:
- Creating safe channels for disclosure.
- Training leaders in trauma awareness.
- Offering practical help such as housing, financial support or advocacy.

- Speaking the truth about abuse rather than hiding behind silence.

When the church acts as the body of Christ, it reflects His compassion and justice.

Closing Thought

Violence seeks to silence women but God calls them by name. Trauma may shape part of their story but it does not define their worth. Healing is possible, dignity can be restored and voices once silenced can rise again.

Reflection & Discussion

1. Where have I carried silence about trauma in my own life or family?
2. How can I create safe spaces for survivors to speak and heal?
3. What scriptures remind me of God's justice and His care for the oppressed?

Scripture for Meditation

- *"The Lord is a refuge for the oppressed, a stronghold in times of trouble." – Psalm 9:9.*
- *"He heals the broken-hearted and binds up their wounds." – Psalm 147:3.*
- *"Rescue the weak and needy; deliver them from the hand of the wicked." – Psalm 82:4.*

PART THREE:
Women Carrying Public and Private Roles

Leadership, marriage, and motherhood bring both honour and hidden costs. This section explores the loneliness of leading, the quiet struggles of ministry wives, the fears of mothers, and the silence around spiritual doubt.

CHAPTER TWELVE

The Lonely Leader – Isolation at the top

> But Jesus often withdrew to lonely places and prayed.
> – LUKE 5:16

Women in leadership bear weight few can see, admired outwardly yet isolated inwardly. This chapter uncovers the hidden cost of authority and the need for safe spaces of support.

1. The Silent Cost of Leadership

From the Old to the New Testament, we see God entrusting women with spiritual authority, prophetic voice and leadership responsibility:
- Deborah served as judge and prophet *(Judges 4–5)*, leading Israel both spiritually and politically.
- Huldah was a prophet whose word authenticated the rediscovered Book of the Law *(2 Kings 22)*.

- Mary Magdalene was the first witness of the resurrection and the first to proclaim it; an apostle to the apostles *(John 20:18)*.
- Priscilla taught Apollos, a learned man, alongside her husband Aquila *(Acts 18:26)*.
- Phoebe was a deacon and benefactor, entrusted by Paul with delivering his epistle to the Romans *(Romans 16:1-2)*.

These are examples of God's inclusion.

Leadership is often admired from the outside but few understand its private cost. Women in leadership whether in church, workplace or community carry a weight of responsibility that can leave them isolated.

I have counselled women who were celebrated publicly yet cried in private, unsure whom they could trust. Every decision was scrutinised, every mistake magnified, every success met with envy. Therefore , their authority brought visibility but also a kind of loneliness no one had prepared them for.

2. Barriers for Women Leaders

Women in leadership face challenges but their male peers often do not. They must prove competence again and again balancing firmness with warmth and authority with approachability. Because they are too assertive, they are labelled as aggressive. Too gentle, they are dismissed as weak. It also seems that in many church cultures, women are more often tolerated in support roles but not empowered to lead, preach, or speak prophetically.

In Christian settings, women leaders may also battle theological opposition. Even when called and gifted, they are questioned simply because they are women. This constant resistance can wear down confidence and create:

This often leads to:
- Spiritual dissonance: "I know I'm called, but I feel out of place."
- Internalised doubt: "Am I being rebellious?"
- Exhaustion: Constantly proving one's worth in male-dominated spaces.
- Isolation: A lack of spiritual mentors, peers, or affirmation.

These are not just leadership challenges, they are soul wounds.

If you are a woman called to lead but weary from the wilderness, know this: You are not disqualified by resistance. You are refined by it. Jesus consistently elevated women's voices and affirmed their dignity and spiritual authority: He defended Mary of Bethany's choice to sit and learn at His feet *(Luke 10:39-42)*. He commissioned the Samaritan woman to evangelize her entire village *(John 4)*. He honoured the woman who anointed Him, saying, "Wherever the gospel is preached... what she has done will be told" *(Mark 14:9)*.

Jesus did not silence women, He released them.

3. The Hidden Strain

Leadership often means carrying others' burdens. Women in positions of influence frequently listen, support and advocate for those they lead. Yet when they themselves struggle, they hesitate to share. Who will listen without gossip? Who will understand without judgement?

The result is hidden exhaustion. Many women pour themselves out until they are empty but silently hoping someone will notice their need for care.

4. Jesus and Solitude

Scripture reminds us that even Jesus withdrew to pray in lonely places. Leadership drew constant demands from the crowds, yet He sought renewal in His Father's presence. His example shows that solitude is not failure but wisdom.

Women in leadership must learn the same rhythm: to serve faithfully but also to step away for rest, reflection, and prayer. Leadership without solitude leads to burnout; solitude with God renews strength.

5. Counselling Pathways

Counselling provides leaders with a rare space where they can be honest without fear of losing credibility. Helpful approaches include:

- **Naming the strain.** Acknowledging loneliness is the first step toward relief.
- **Encouraging healthy boundaries.** Leadership does not mean being available at all times.
- **Affirming identity beyond role.** A leader is not defined by title or position but by being a child of God.
- **Exploring support systems.** Building networks of trusted peers, mentors, or counsellors helps break isolation.

6. The Church's Call

Churches and faith communities must do more to support women in leadership. This means:
- Affirming their call with the same seriousness as men's.
- Offering mentoring and peer support.
- Teaching congregations to respect authority without gender bias.
- Encouraging leaders to rest without guilt.

A healthy church honours both the strength and the humanity of its leaders.

Closing Thought

Leadership brings responsibility but it should not bring isolation. Women called to lead must be supported not left to carry their burdens in silence. God does not ask His daughters to lead alone but He provides community and His own presence as refuge.

The loneliness of leadership can be eased when women know they are seen, heard, and valued not only for what they give but for who they are.

Reflection & Discussion

1. Where have I experienced the loneliness of leadership in my own life?
2. What practices help me stay rooted in God when responsibilities feel heavy?
3. How can churches and communities better support women in leadership?
4. Who can I trust to walk with me honestly in seasons of strain?

Scripture for Meditation

- *"But Jesus often withdrew to lonely places and prayed."* - Luke 5:16.
- *"The Lord is my shepherd, I lack nothing."* - Psalm 23:1.
- *"Come with me by yourselves to a quiet place and get some rest."* - Mark 6:31.

CHAPTER THIRTEEN

Behind the Pulpit Wife's Smile: Ministry marriages under pressure

> ❝ *Two are better than one, because they have a good return for their labour: if either of them falls down, one can help the other up.*
> – ECCLESIASTES 4:9-10 ❞

The wife of a leader is often expected to be flawless: prayerful, patient, ever-present. This chapter reveals the private struggles behind ministry marriages and the pressure to perform.

1. The Ideal and the Reality

Marriage is often pictured as companionship, love and mutual support. In Christian ministry, it is sometimes portrayed as the perfect partnership, husband and wife serving side by side in harmony.

Church; the place where many come to find healing, comfort and belonging, can sometimes be the very space where a woman's pain is most overlooked. While hymns are sung and hands are raised, silent battles rage behind the pews and pulpits alike.

Leah, a 42-year-old deaconess, sat across from me with folded arms and tired eyes.

"I love my church," she said. "But I've never felt lonelier."

Her voice trembled. "I lead worship, teach Bible studies, and I'm the first to respond when someone is in crisis but when I went through my own miscarriage... no one noticed I disappeared for three weeks. Not one person called."

Her silence had gone unnoticed, or worse ignored.

Behind the public image, many wives carry hidden struggles. They uphold appearances for the sake of family or ministry while inside they feel unseen, unsupported or alone. The expectation to be a "model wife" can become a mask that hides deep weariness.

2. The Silent Pressure of Ministry Wives

Wives of pastors, elders or church leaders are often placed under expectations they never chose. They are expected to host, serve, pray, encourage and remain composed at all times. When cracks appear in their marriages, they may feel they cannot speak, fearing it will damage their husband's reputation or the church's image.

This silence leaves many women isolated. They carry the weight of private disappointment while being praised publicly for their strength. Their silence isn't because they have no voice, it's because the environment they serve in has little room for their vulnerability.

3. The Struggles Behind Closed Doors

- **Loneliness:** Ministry commitments can leave little time for intimacy or family connection.
- **Unmet needs:** Emotional, spiritual or physical needs may go unacknowledged.
- **Lack of voice:** Decisions are made without their input even when those decisions affect them directly.
- **Hidden conflict:** Disagreements are suppressed to protect appearances leaving resentment to grow.

One wife confided, "I am celebrated on Sunday but forgotten on Monday." Her words captured the gulf between public honour and private neglect.

Maria, a 55-year-old intercessory leader, had been battling clinical depression for nearly a decade. Her church offered prayer but no pastoral follow-up, viewing her mental illness as a spiritual weakness rather than a medical and emotional reality. She was told to 'pray more' and 'rebuke the spirit of heaviness,'" she said. "But no one ever asked me how I was actually coping. It made me feel like a failure.

Her story is not rare. Many women in the church internalise a sense of guilt when their emotional needs are not met with empathy but rather with correction. They are taught to serve, but not always permitted to struggle.

4. The Mask of Faith

Many wives are told to endure silently, quoting verses about patience and submission. Faith becomes tied to silence as if speaking honestly would dishonour God. Yet true faith is not pretending. The *Psalms* show us that lament, protest and honesty are part of worship.

Jesus Himself rebuked religious leaders who prioritised appearance over truth. He valued integrity more than image. For wives in ministry, honesty before God and in trusted spaces is not rebellion but it is freedom.

5. Counselling and Healing

Counselling provides a safe place for ministry wives to remove the mask. Helpful steps include:
- Validating their experience. Pain is real even when hidden behind public success.

- Exploring identity. They are more than "the pastor's wife." They are daughters of God gifted and valuable in their own right.
- Encouraging honest dialogue. Healing begins when couples learn to speak truthfully about their needs and struggles.
- Supporting self-care. Time for rest, friendships and personal growth strengthens both wife and marriage.

6. A Call to the Church

Churches must care for ministry wives not as extensions of their husbands but as individuals. This means:
- Respecting their privacy and boundaries.
- Offering support without expectations of unpaid labour.
- Encouraging them to use their own gifts apart from their husband's role.
- Recognising that their wellbeing is vital for the health of the whole family.

Closing Thought

Marriage and ministry are not meant to be prisons of performance. God's design is partnership, honesty and mutual care. Wives should not have to hide their struggles to protect appearances. When their voices are valued and their needs honoured, both marriage and ministry become spaces of grace.

Reflection & Discussion

1. How have cultural or church expectations shaped the way wives in ministry are seen?
2. What hidden struggles might a wife carry while maintaining a public image?
3. How can churches become places where ministry families are cared for honestly, not idealised?
4. How might honesty in marriage reflect God's truth more than silence does?

Scripture for Meditation

- *"Two are better than one, if either of them falls down, one can help the other up." - Ecclesiastes 4:9- 10.*
- *"Speak the truth in love, so that we will grow to become in every respect the mature body of Him who is the head, that is, Christ." - Ephesians 4:15.*
- *"The Lord is close to the broken-hearted." - Psalm 34:18.*

CHAPTER FOURTEEN

Motherhood's Quiet Fears:
The hidden weight of raising children

> Train up a child in the way he should go,
> and when he is old he will not depart from it.
> – PROVERBS 22:6

Motherhood is a blessing but also a burden of worry and expectation. Here we name the silent fears mothers carry about adequacy, judgement and their children's futures.

1. The Hidden Weight of Motherhood

Motherhood is often celebrated as a blessing, yet many mothers carry hidden fears and unspoken pressures. They wonder if they are raising their children well, if they are doing enough or if their mistakes will leave lasting scars.

Behind warm smiles and busy routines, mothers often lie awake at night, questioning their adequacy. They worry about providing, guiding, protecting and nurturing while rarely admitting how heavy this calling can feel.

2. Cultural and Community Expectations

Different cultures place immense pressure on mothers. In African contexts, a woman's worth is often tied to how well her children behave, excel in school, or marry respectably. In Western settings, mothers are measured by their ability to balance career and family seamlessly.

Churches too can add pressure. Sermons on the *Proverbs 31* woman sometimes become a burden rather than an encouragement. Instead of drawing strength, many mothers hear only that they fall short.

These expectations create a silent competition where mothers compare themselves and secretly fear that they are failing.

3. The Quiet Fears Mothers Carry

- **Fear of inadequacy:** "Am I doing enough for my children?"
- **Fear of judgement:** "What will people think if my child struggles?"

- **Fear of loss:** "What if I cannot protect them from harm?"
- **Fear of the future:** "Will they grow in faith, or drift away?"

These questions weigh heavily, especially when mothers have little space to voice them.

4. Biblical Mothers Who Struggled

Scripture itself acknowledges the struggle of motherhood. Hannah wept bitterly for a child and later entrusted Samuel to God's service. Mary the mother of Jesus faced misunderstanding, danger and the grief of watching her son suffer.

Their stories remind us that faithful mothers are not perfect mothers. However , they are women who brought their fears and hopes before God.

5. Counselling Pathways

When mothers share their pressures in counselling, the work is often to create space for honesty without shame. Helpful steps include:
- **Normalising fear.** Worry does not mean failure but reveals love.
- **Releasing perfection.** No mother can meet every need. God's grace fills what we cannot.

- **Encouraging support systems.** Parenting was never meant to be done alone.
- **Integrating faith.** Prayer and scripture become anchors not standards of judgement.

6. The Church's Role

Churches can ease mothers' burdens by:
- Providing practical help like childcare, meals and community support.
- Offering safe spaces for honest conversation about struggles.
- Teaching parenting as stewardship not performance.
- Celebrating mothers for who they are not only for what they do.

Closing Thought

Motherhood is holy work but it is also exhausting work. God does not demand perfection from mothers but He invites them to lean on His strength. The same God who entrusted children to their care also promises to carry both mother and child.

Reflection & Discussion

1. What quiet fears do I carry as a mother, aunt or caregiver?
2. How have cultural or church expectations shaped my parenting journey?
3. Where might I need to release perfection and trust God with my children?
4. How can communities better support mothers in practical and spiritual ways?

Scripture for Meditation

- *"Train up a child in the way he should go, and when he is old he will not depart from it." - Proverbs 22:6.*
- *"He tends His flock like a shepherd: He gathers the lambs in His arms and carries them close balance to His heart; He gently leads those that are young." - Isaiah 40:11.*
- *"Do not worry about tomorrow, for tomorrow will worry about itself." - Matthew 6:34.*

CHAPTER FIFTEEN

Faith Under Fire: Spiritual doubt and silence in Christian life

> ❝ *My God, my God, why have You forsaken me?*
> – MATTHEW 27:46 ❞

Many women hide spiritual dryness, anger or unanswered questions. This chapter validates those struggles, reminding us that even doubt and lament can be forms of faith.

1. The Silence Around Spiritual Struggle

In Christian communities, faith is often spoken of in terms of certainty, joy, and strength. Doubt, anger at God, or spiritual dryness are rarely voiced. Many women feel they must appear unwavering in their faith even when inside they feel abandoned, confused or numb.

I have counselled women who pray faithfully yet confess that their prayers feel empty. Others serve tirelessly in church while privately wondering if God hears them at all. Their struggle is real but silence surrounds it.

2. Why Women Stay Silent

- **Fear of judgement:** They worry that admitting doubt will make others question their salvation.
- **Pressure to perform:** In families and churches, women are often expected to be the spiritual anchors, holding everyone else together.
- **Cultural conditioning:** In many African and diaspora settings, questioning God is viewed as dishonour. Silence becomes the safer option.

Yet silence prolongs the struggle hence leaving women spiritually exhausted.

3. Faith Tested in Scripture

The Bible does not hide spiritual struggle.
- Job cursed the day of his birth and demanded answers from God.
- Hannah poured out her grief so deeply that Eli thought she was drunk.
- David's psalms swing between despair and praise, sometimes in the same breath.

- Even Jesus cried out in anguish on the cross: *"My God, my God, why have You forsaken me?"*

These examples remind us that struggle is part of faith, not the opposite of it. God welcomes honesty more than performance.

4. The Impact of Hidden Struggle

When women suppress spiritual struggles, the effects are profound:
- **Isolation:** They feel alone in their doubt.
- **Guilt:** They believe their questions make them bad Christians.
- **Burnout:** Continued service without spiritual renewal leads to exhaustion.

Over time, this silence can erode confidence in God's love, creating distance rather than intimacy.

5. Counselling Pathways

In counselling, women wrestling with faith need space to express doubts without fear. Healing begins when they hear that questions are not signs of failure but steps toward deeper faith. Practical support includes:
- **Validating honesty.** Reminding them God invites lament and welcomes questions.

- **Encouraging spiritual rest.** Releasing the pressure to perform. Prayer can be a silent presence, not only words.
- **Reframing faith.** Struggle can refine rather than destroying belief.
- **Integrating scripture.** Use psalms of lament as prayers when personal words fail.

6. The Role of the Church

Churches must normalise conversations about spiritual struggle. This means:
- Preaching on biblical characters who wrestled with God.
- Encouraging testimonies that include valleys as well as mountaintops.
- Creating groups where women can share honestly without fear of being judged.

When churches model honesty, women are freed from silence and find companionship in their struggles.

Closing Thought

Faith under fire is not faith lost. The presence of doubt, despair or silence does not mean God is absent. He remains faithful even when our feelings say otherwise.

A woman may feel like her faith is barely a flicker, yet *Isaiah 42:3 promises: "A bruised reed He will not break, and a smouldering wick He will not snuff out."* God holds her gently until her flame is strong again.

Reflection & Discussion

1. What spiritual struggles have I hidden for fear of being judged?
2. How do stories of Job, Hannah, David, or Jesus reshape my view of faith in hard times?
3. Who in my life can I trust with my doubts and questions?
4. How can my church become a safer place for honest spiritual struggle?

Scripture for Meditation

- *"My God, my God, why have You forsaken me?" - Matthew 27:46.*
- *"The Lord is close to the broken-hearted and saves those who are crushed in spirit." - Psalm 34:18.*
- *"A bruised reed He will not break, and a smouldering wick He will not snuff out." - Isaiah 42:3.*

PART FOUR:
Seasons of Womanhood

Every life stage brings unique challenges; singleness misunderstood, widowhood overlooked, ageing dismissed, daughters pressed by digital culture and churches failing to protect. Here, we give voice to women across generations and cultures.

CHAPTER SIXTEEN

Single, Not Silent: Misconceptions about unmarried women

> " *I have learned to be content whatever the circumstances.*
> – PHILIPPIANS 4:11 "

Singleness is too often treated as a deficiency. This chapter reclaims the single life as purposeful and whole, challenging stereotypes within culture and church.

1. The Weight of Expectations

In many cultures, a woman's worth is measured by her marital status. A single woman, no matter how accomplished, may be treated as incomplete. Families whisper, church members pray for her to "find someone," and society assumes she must be waiting for marriage to validate her life.

I have counselled women in their thirties, forties, and beyond who thrive in careers and ministries yet feel diminished because they are not married. The silence surrounding their struggles is not about the absence of marriage itself but about the constant message that they are less because of it.

2. Cultural and Church Pressures

- **Family expectations:** In African families, questions about marriage often begin in a woman's twenties and rarely stop. A delay in marriage can invite pity, gossip or intrusive advice.
- **Church assumptions:** Unmarried women are often viewed as projects to be fixed rather than individuals to be celebrated. They may be excluded from leadership or seen as spiritually lacking.
- **Social stigma:** In wider society, singleness may carry labels of being "too picky," "too difficult," or "not desirable."

These pressures create an environment where unmarried women feel silenced and unseen, even in communities that should affirm them.

3. The Internal Struggle

Silence around singleness leaves many women battling unspoken fears:
- *Am I unwanted?*
- *Will I grow old alone?*
- *Has God forgotten me?*
- *Do I still have value if I never marry?*

Such questions cut deeply, particularly when unanswered year after year. Some women settle in unhealthy relationships to avoid stigma while others retreat from community to escape constant reminders.

4. Biblical Witness

The Bible honours singleness. Jesus Himself lived a single life, fully human and fully fulfilled. Paul spoke of singleness as a gift offering freedom for service *(1 Corinthians 7:7)*. Women such as Mary Magdalene and Lydia shaped the early church not through marriage but through devotion and leadership.

Singleness is not absence. It is presence, the presence of gifts, calling and identity in Christ.

5. Counselling Pathways

In counselling, supporting unmarried women involves:
- **Affirming identity.** Reminding them that their worth is not defined by marital status.
- **Addressing grief.** For those who longed for marriage or children, space must be made for lament.
- **Encouraging purpose.** Explore passions, callings and contributions that bring life and meaning.
- **Challenging stigma.** Equip women to respond to intrusive comments with confidence and grace.

6. The Church's Call

Churches must learn to honour single women as complete and valuable members of the body of Christ. This means:
- Including them in leadership not only in service roles.
- Celebrating their gifts and contributions without reducing their identity to marital status.
- Offering pastoral care that sees them as a whole not lacking.

Closing Thought

Singleness is not a deficiency. It is a season sometimes chosen, sometimes not but always held in God's hands. Every woman, married or single is fully loved and fully valuable in His sight.

The silence around unmarried women must end. Their voices, gifts and presence are vital to the church and the world.

Reflection & Discussion

1. How have cultural or church expectations shaped my view of singleness?
2. What silent struggles have I carried as an unmarried woman, or witnessed in others?
3. How can communities affirm single women as whole and valued?
4. What scriptures remind me of God's love and purpose beyond marital status?

Scripture for Meditation
- "I have learned to be content whatever the circumstances." - Philippians 4:11.
- "The unmarried woman cares about the things of the Lord, that she may be holy both in body and in spirit." - 1 Corinthians 7:34.
- "You are complete in Him, who is the head over every power and authority." - Colossians 2:10.

CHAPTER SEVENTEEN

Widows in the Shadows: Grief, invisibility and resilience

> " A father to the fatherless, a defender of widows,
> is God in His holy dwelling.
> – PSALM 68:5 "

Widowhood brings loss of spouse, identity and community standing. This chapter addresses the layered grief and cultural neglect widows endure and God's promise to defend them.

1. The Lonely Silence

Widowhood is one of the heaviest transitions a woman can face. It is not only the loss of a husband but also the loss of identity, companionship and often community standing. Many widows speak of feeling invisible as though their presence matters less without a partner beside them.

Some are met with pity, others with suspicion and some with avoidance as if widowhood is contagious. The silence around their grief can deepen isolation.

2. Cultural Burdens

In many cultures, widows face painful traditions. Some are forced to undergo degrading rituals to "prove innocence" in their husband's death. Others are stripped of property or denied inheritance rights. In some African families, a widow may be pressured to marry a relative of her late husband regardless of her wishes.

These customs compound grief with injustice most especially, treating widows as burdens rather than women deserving dignity.

3. Church and Community Gaps

Even within churches, widows may be overlooked. Support is often strong in the first days after a funeral, then fades as life returns to normal for others. The widow remains facing empty nights and financial strain while trying to navigate a new identity she never asked for.

Yet scripture repeatedly commands care for widows. In Deuteronomy, God instructs His people to include them in festivals and provision whilst in the New Testament widows are honoured for their prayers and faith but God Himself is described as their defender.

4. The Inner Struggles of Widowhood

Widows carry fears that are often unspoken:
- *How will I survive financially?*
- *Will I always feel this lonely?*
- *Who am I now without my husband?*
- *Does anyone still see me?*

These questions touch not only practical needs but also the soul.

5. Counselling Pathways

Counselling for widows involves creating space for both grief and rebuilding. Key approaches include:
- **Permission to grieve.** Grief does not follow a timetable. It may resurface unexpectedly for years.
- **Rebuilding identity.** Encourage widows to rediscover who they are as individuals, gifted and valued in God's sight.
- **Addressing practical needs.** Support in navigating finances, legal matters and community roles is essential.
- **Restoring community.** Loneliness eases when safe networks of support and friendship are rebuilt.

6. The Church's Role

Churches can reflect God's heart for widows by:
- Offering consistent pastoral and practical support long after the funeral.
- Challenging harmful cultural practices that exploit or demean widows.
- Inviting widows into leadership and ministry by not relegating them to the margins.
- Speaking openly of God's promise to defend and honour them.

Closing Thought

Widowhood is not the end of a woman's story. Though loss is profound, God promises to be her defender and sustainer. He sees what others overlook and calls her precious still.

A widow may feel invisible but to God she is never unseen.

Reflection & Discussion

1. What cultural or personal assumptions about widowhood have I witnessed?
2. How can I or my community stand with widows in practical, ongoing ways?
3. What does it mean to believe that God Himself is a defender of widows?

Scripture for Meditation

- "A father to the fatherless, a defender of widows, is God in His holy dwelling." - Psalm 68:5.
- "The religion that God our Father accepts as pure and faultless is this: to look after orphans and widows in their distress." - James 1:27.
- "The Lord watches over the foreigner and sustains the fatherless and the widow." - Psalm 146:9.

CHAPTER EIGHTEEN

Growing Older, Growing Stronger: Ageing and the fear of irrelevance

> *Even to your old age and grey hairs I am He,*
> *I am He who will sustain you. I have made you and I will*
> *carry you; I will sustain you and I will rescue you.*
> – ISAIAH 46:4

Older women carry wisdom yet often feel discarded in a youth-obsessed world. Here we affirm ageing not as obsolescence but as a season of fruitfulness and legacy.

1. The Quiet Fear of Becoming Irrelevant

Aging is a natural part of life, yet for many women it brings fear: fear of being overlooked, excluded or dismissed as no longer useful. In cultures that idolise youth and productivity, older women often feel invisible.

I have listened to women in their sixties and seventies who speak of deep wisdom gained through life's journey, yet they also share the pain of being pushed aside as if their contribution has expired. Their silence hides not a lack of thought, but the fear that no one wishes to hear it.

2. Cultural and Societal Pressures

- **In some African families,** older women are valued for their wisdom but may also face expectations to care endlessly for grandchildren, often without recognition or support.
- **In Western settings,** older women may face workplace discrimination, forced into early retirement or passed over for advancement.
- **In wider society,** ageing bodies are ridiculed and beauty is equated with youth.

These pressures combine to convince many women that they are no longer significant.

3. The Inner Struggles of Aging

The journey of aging brings questions that are rarely voiced aloud:
- *Who am I when my children no longer need me?*
- *Do I still matter when my body slows down?*
- *What is my place in a world that celebrates the young?*

Some women fear becoming burdens. Others wrestle with regrets or unfulfilled dreams. The silence surrounding these fears intensifies their loneliness.

4. Biblical Witness of Older Women

Scripture honours aging women. Anna the prophetess served faithfully into her eighties recognising the infant Christ in the temple *(Luke 2:36-38)*. Naomi though grieving and bitter, became part of God's redemption story through Ruth. Older women are also entrusted in *Titus 2:3-5* to guide younger generations with wisdom.

In God's story, age is not obsolescence. It is fruitfulness in another form.

5. Counselling Pathways

Counselling older women means affirming both their grief and their ongoing purpose. Helpful approaches include:
- **Validating their voice.** Their stories carry wisdom that should be honoured.
- **Exploring legacy.** Supporting them in seeing the impact of their lives on family, church and the community.
- **Addressing loss.** Space to grieve health changes, widowhood or diminished roles is essential.

- **Encouraging new purpose.** Aging can be a time of mentoring, creativity and spiritual deepening.

6. The Church's Responsibility

Churches must resist the cultural idolisation of youth by honouring older women as vital members of the body. This includes:
- Inviting them into leadership, prayer and teaching roles.
- Creating intergenerational spaces where wisdom is shared.
- Supporting them practically in health, housing and companionship.
- Celebrating their presence as a gift not a burden.

Closing Thought

Aging does not make a woman obsolete. Though her role may change, her values do not. In God's eyes, she remains beloved, chosen and purposeful. He promises to carry her into old age, sustaining her life until the end.

The world may turn away from older women, but God leans in closer.

Reflection & Discussion

1. What silent fears have I carried about aging and relevance?
2. How do I view older women in my family, church, or workplace?
3. What legacy do I hope to leave, and how can I begin shaping it now?
4. How can my community celebrate and include the voices of older women?

Scripture for Meditation

- *"Even to your old age and grey hairs I am He, I am He who will sustain you."* - Isaiah 46:4.
- *"The righteous will flourish like a palm tree... they will still bear fruit in old age."* - Psalm 92:12-14.
- *"Gray hair is a crown of splendour; it is attained in the way of righteousness."* - Proverbs 16:31.

CHAPTER NINETEEN

Daughters Under Pressure:
Young women in a digital age

> ❝
> *Don't let anyone look down on you because you are young, but set an example for the believers in speech, conduct, love, faith and in purity.*
> – 1 TIMOTHY 4:12
> ❞

Girls and young women face crushing expectations from family, peers and social media. This chapter voices their hidden anxieties and calls for mentoring and safe spaces.

1. The Silent Struggles of Youth

Young women today navigate a world of immense pressure. They face expectations from family, demands from education or work and constant comparisons fuelled by social media. Many are struggling with identity, anxiety or loneliness, yet they suffer quietly.

In counselling, I often hear the voices of young women who feel unheard at home, unseen in church and misunderstood by society. They mask their distress with smiles, achievements or online personas but underneath lies fear and confusion.

2. Pressures That Crush

- **Family expectations:** In many African and diaspora communities, daughters are expected to excel academically, uphold family reputation and prepare for **marriage all at once.**
- **Peer and social pressures:** Social media fuels comparison, leaving young women feeling inadequate about appearance, lifestyle or success.
- **Church pressures:** Young women are often expected to embody purity and service but may be silenced if they raise questions or express doubt.

These overlapping demands can overwhelm leaving them isolated in their pain.

3. The Inner Voices of Distress

The silence of young women is filled with unspoken questions:
- *Am I good enough?*
- *Why don't I look like her?*
- *Do I matter in my family, in church, in the world?*
- *Is God disappointed in me?*

Without safe spaces to process these questions, many turn to unhealthy coping: withdrawal, disordered eating, risky relationships or hidden addictions.

4. Biblical Daughters Who Struggled

Scripture does not ignore the cries of the young. Dinah suffered injustice and silence *(Genesis 34)*. Tamar's trauma was dismissed by her family *(2 Samuel 13)*. Yet we also see Mary, a young woman entrusted with the incarnation itself, whose faith and courage changed history.

These stories remind us that God sees daughters in distress. He does not dismiss their pain. He calls them valuable, purposeful, and beloved.

5. Counselling Pathways

Supporting young women means listening without judgement and validating their struggles. Counselling approaches include:
- **Affirming identity.** Helping them see themselves as more than achievements or appearances.
- **Addressing mental health.** Creating space for conversations about anxiety, depression and self-harm without stigma.
- **Encouraging healthy boundaries.** Equipping them to resist harmful pressures and comparisons.

- **Integrating faith.** Teach them that God welcomes honesty, questions and vulnerability.

6. The Role of Families and Churches

Families must learn to hear their daughters' voices, not just their achievements. Churches must become safe places where young women can ask difficult questions, lead with their gifts and be discipled with patience and grace.

Practical steps include:
- Mentorship programmes pairing younger women with older trusted mentors.
- Honest teaching about identity, sexuality and faith that avoids shame.
- Spaces for creative expression and service that affirms their value.

Closing Thought

Young women should not have to suffer in silence. Their questions, struggles and hopes are precious to God. He calls them to be examples in love, faith and purity not because they are perfect, but because His Spirit works powerfully in them.

When we listen to daughters in distress and lift their voices, we help them step into the fullness of who God created them to be.

Reflection & Discussion

1. What unspoken struggles have I carried or witnessed in young women around me?
2. How has social, cultural or church pressure shaped the way I see myself or others?
3. Who could I mentor, listen to or encourage in their journey of faith?
4. What scriptures remind me that God values young women fully and deeply?

Scripture for Meditation

- *"Don't let anyone look down on you because you are young..." - 1 Timothy 4:12.*
- *"You are precious and honoured in My sight, and because I love you." - Isaiah 43:4.*
- *"Before I formed you in the womb I knew you, before you were born I set you apart." - Jeremiah 1:5.*

CHAPTER TWENTY

When the Church is Silent: Failures of faith communities to protect women

> **"**
> Speak up and judge fairly; defend the rights of the poor and needy.
> – PROVERBS 31:9
> **"**

Churches should be sanctuaries, yet many perpetuate silence by minimising abuse or restricting women's voices. This chapter challenges the church to embody Christ's justice and compassion.

1. The Wound of Silence

Churches should be places of refuge, yet too often they become places of silence. Women bring their struggles, abuse, infertility, depression, grief, only to find their pain minimised or ignored. The silence of the sanctuary does not heal; it deepens wounds.

I have counselled women who were told to stay in abusive marriages to protect the church's image or urged to forgive without accountability. Others were excluded from leadership because of their gender no matter their gifts. The very community meant to embody Christ's compassion became another source of suffering.

2. When the Church Protects Image Over People

Churches sometimes prioritise reputation over truth. Leaders hush allegations of abuse to avoid scandal. Families are encouraged to "keep it private" rather than seek justice. Women who speak out are labelled divisive or unspiritual.

This culture of silence betrays the gospel. Jesus never protected the powerful at the expense of the vulnerable. He confronted hypocrisy and defended the marginalised. A church that silences women fails to reflect His heart.

3. Misuse of Teaching

Some church teachings when misapplied, create an environment where women are silenced:
- Submission is taught without the balance of mutual love.
- Purity is emphasised without grace, leaving women ashamed of their bodies.
- Service is praised while rest and self-care are condemned as selfish.

The result is women are burdened, silenced and overlooked in the very place that should lift them.

4. God's Vision for His Church

The New Testament reveals a different vision:
- Women such as Priscilla, Phoebe, Junia and Lydia played vital roles in the early church.
- *Galatians 3:28 declares that in Christ there is neither male nor female, for all are one in Him.*
- The church is called the bride of Christ that is cherished and honoured.

In God's design, women are not second-class members but co-labourers in His kingdom.

5. A Pastoral and Prophetic Response

When churches fail women, the response must be both pastoral and prophetic:
- **Pastoral:** Offer healing to those hurt by the church, affirming that God's love is not reflected in their mistreatment. Provide spaces for lament and rebuilding of trust.
- **Prophetic:** Call churches to repentance where silence has enabled harm. Challenge leaders to prioritise people over image, truth over convenience and justice over reputation.

6. Practical Steps for Churches

- Create safe safeguarding systems for reporting abuse.
- Train leaders in trauma awareness and gender sensitivity.
- Preach the full truth of scripture and also honour women as equal partners in God's work.
- Celebrate women's gifts by giving them space to lead, teach and serve without restriction.

A church that listens and honours women reflects the kingdom of God more truthfully than one that silences them.

Closing Thought

The sanctuary is meant to be a place of healing, not harm. When churches silence women, they distort the gospel. But when churches listen, protect and empower, they become the living body of Christ and a refuge where all find dignity and grace.

Reflection & Discussion

1. Where have I seen or experienced silence in the church that harmed women?
2. How has my own faith been shaped by the way churches treat women?
3. What changes would help the church reflect Christ's love more faithfully?

4. How can I use my voice to speak truth within my community of faith?

Scripture for Meditation

- *"Speak up and judge fairly; defend the rights of the poor and needy." - Proverbs 31:9.*
- *"There is neither Jew nor Gentile, slave nor free, nor is there male and female, for you are all one in Christ Jesus." - Galatians 3:28.*
- *"The Lord is a refuge for the oppressed, a stronghold in times of trouble." - Psalm 9:9.*

PART FIVE:
Breaking Silence, Finding Wholeness

The final section turns from exposure to restoration. It calls women, families, churches and communities to name hidden pain, confront injustice and embrace God's vision for healing, dignity and wholeness in Christ.

CHAPTER TWENTY-ONE

Breaking Silence: Finding Wholeness

> ❝
> He heals the broken-hearted and binds up their wounds.
> – PSALM 147:3
> ❞

Healing begins when pain is named. This closing chapter gathers the threads of hidden struggles, offering a vision of wholeness through honesty, community and Christ's redemptive love.

1. The Power of Naming- From secrecy to voice

Throughout these chapters, we have looked at many forms of silence around menstruation and menopause, hidden illness, mental health struggles, abuse, shame, widowhood and the burdens women carry in families, workplaces and churches.

Silence allows suffering to grow unchecked. Naming pain is the beginning of healing. When women speak their truth, when families listen, when churches respond with compassion as a result, the cycle of hidden wounds begins to break.

2. God's Heart for Wholeness

The God of scripture is not distant from women's pain. He sees Hagar in the wilderness and becomes the *"God who sees" (Genesis 16:13)*. He honours the faith of the bleeding woman who reached for His garment *(Luke 8:48)*. He weeps at the tomb with Mary and Martha *(John 11:35)*.

God is not threatened by our tears or silence. He enters it, sits with us and transforms it into hope. His desire is for the wholeness of the body, mind and the spirit.

3. The Role of Counselling and Community

Counselling creates space to voice what has long been hidden. It validates women's stories and helps them integrate faith with healing. Yet counselling alone is not enough, Communities must also change.
- **Families** must stop shaming daughters and begin affirming them.
- **Churches** must preach the full counsel of scripture by honouring women's voices and experiences.

- **Society** must challenge stereotypes and systems that diminish women.

Wholeness comes when silence is broken collectively.

4. Towards a New Culture of Honesty

Breaking the silence means choosing honesty over image. It means creating spaces where women can say, *"I am not okay"* without fear of judgement. It means replacing secrecy with compassion and stigma with truth.

The early church was marked by honesty and shared burdens *(Acts 2:42-47)*. When women and men alike confess struggles, pray together and carry one another's loads, healing becomes possible.

5. A Call to Women

To the women reading this: your story matters. Your voice carries weight. You are not invisible to God and you should not be invisible to His people. Whether you are young or old, married or single, thriving or struggling, be assured that your life is precious.

Do not let shame or silence steal your dignity. In Christ, you are fully known and fully loved.

6. A Call to the Church

To the church: listen to your daughters, sisters, mothers and widows. Believe them when they speak. Honour their gifts, defend their safety and create sanctuaries where women find not silence but support, not dismissal but dignity.

When the church embraces women as equal partners in the kingdom, it reflects the heart of Christ more fully.

Closing Thought

Silence has wounded many women but it does not have the final word. However , Christ does. He is the healer of broken hearts, the defender of the oppressed and the restorer of dignity.

May this book be a step toward breaking the silence, naming the hidden pain and walking together toward wholeness in Him.

Reflection & Discussion

1. What silence in my own life still needs to be broken?
2. How can I support other women in speaking their truth?

3. In what ways can my church or community become a place of healing rather than harm?
4. How does Christ's compassion reshape the way I see myself and others?

Scripture for Meditation

- *"He heals the broken-hearted and binds up their wounds." - Psalm 147:3.*
- *"You are the God who sees me." - Genesis 16:13.*
- *"Carry each other's burdens, and in this way you will fulfil the law of Christ." - Galatians 6:2*
- *"The truth will set you free." - John 8:32.*

EPILOGUE:

Let the Silence Be Broken

> " There is a time to be silent and a time to speak.
> – ECCLESIASTES 3:7 "

There is a silence that screams.

It hides behind the choir robe, kitchen counters, conference pulpits and the prayer circle. It wears lipstick and raises children. It leads worship , shows up week after week, but beneath the smile lies an ache that has never been named.

This book is for her.
- For the woman who greets warmly at the church door but cries on the way home.
- For the one who holds everyone else together while quietly falling apart.
- For the one who has learned to suffer in silence because history, family or faith told her that vulnerability was unsafe or worse and unacceptable.

Over more than two decades as a Christian counsellor, I have sat across from women who have mastered the art of hiding. Some have buried trauma so deeply that they forgot it themselves. Others silenced their voices to preserve peace in marriages, churches or families. Some hid depression beneath devotion, shame beneath scripture and pain behind performance.

But silence left unhealed festers and that is the heartbeat of this book: to give language to what has long remained unspoken.

1. Why This Book Now?

For too long, the Church has celebrated women's strength without making space for their struggle.

We have applauded service while ignoring suffering.
We have quoted Proverbs 31 while overlooking Psalm 31.
The psalm of the woman whose soul is in anguish and whose bones waste away with sorrow.

It is time to listen to the stories we have overlooked.
It is time to bring what has been hidden into the healing light of Christ.

2. Naming the Invisible, Uniting for Change

Throughout this journey, we have uncovered the hidden battles women face:
- Menstruation and menopause cloaked in stigma.
- Chronic conditions, endometriosis, fibromyalgia, PCOS and fibroids have been dismissed as "in your head."
- Singleness misunderstood as incompleteness.
- Emotional labour and caregiving carried without recognition.
- Workplace wounds: microaggressions, the motherhood penalty, unspoken discrimination.
- Reproductive autonomy eroded by judgement and silence.
- Cultural cages of honour, shame and systemic neglect.
- Traditions such as bride price trapping women in harmful marriages.

These struggles are not isolated. They form a tapestry of neglect and misunderstanding. Yet, woven through all of them is a thread of hope.

The very act of naming pain is the first step toward healing. To name it is to shine light into darkness, to challenge myths and injustices that thrive in the shadows. Naming declares that these hidden battles matter, that the women who fight them deserve recognition, care, justice and healing.

But naming is only the beginning. Healing requires solidarity. Women must stand together across cultures, classes, marital statuses and faith communities. And solidarity must grow into action for real change in churches, healthcare systems, workplaces and society at large. Women's bodies, minds, hearts and voices must be honoured as God intended.

3. A Sacred Charge

As Christian counsellors, pastors and leaders, our calling is clear:
- To create spaces where women can tell their stories without shame.
- To confront cultural and systemic injustice with wisdom and grace.
- To empower women to live in the freedom Christ has already secured.

The road ahead demands courage, unity and faith. It demands that we refuse to accept silence as the final word.

> *"Speak up for those who cannot speak for themselves, for the rights of all who are destitute. Speak up and judge fairly; defend the rights of the poor and needy."*
> – PROVERBS 31:8–9

4. Final Word: The Silence Stops Here

This book is written for every woman who has smiled while breaking inside, for every pastor's wife who has hidden her tears, for every leader who has wondered if her story disqualifies her and for every girl who has been told that her worth depends on silence.

To you I say: the silence stops here.

If you have ever asked, *"Is it okay not to be okay?"* Yes, it is.
If you have ever wondered, *"Does God see this part of me?"* Yes, He sees, and He loves you still.
If you have ever feared, *"Is my story too messy for ministry?"* No, it is not. God redeems even this.

My prayer is that as you close these pages, something long buried will rise. That healing will meet you not only in your habits but in your history. That you will discover the liberating truth: you do not have to whisper what God is willing to redeem.

Let us journey together from silence to speech, from shame to strength and from hiddenness to healing.

With grace and truth.

Dr. Olivia Winner, PhD
Christian Counsellor, Marriage, Families and Child Therapy

CLOSING DEVOTIONAL PRAYER – FROM SILENCE TO HEALING

Jesus, Wonderful Counsellor, thank You for hearing what has long been hidden. Give us communities that protect the vulnerable, leaders who listen and homes where dignity is safe. Bind up the brokenhearted and crown women with joy instead of shame. Amen.

GLOSSARY OF KEY TERMS

Reader's Note: How to Use This Glossary

This glossary is here to support your journey through the book. Some of the struggles women face are best named with the language of psychology, while others come alive through the language of Scripture. Together, these words help us see what was hidden, speak what was silenced, and find language for our healing.

Don't feel pressure to memorise them. Instead, dip in whenever you come across a term you'd like to understand more deeply. Let the short definitions give clarity and let the scriptures breathe hope into your heart.

Clinical & Psychological Terms

Emotional Labour
The unseen effort of managing emotions and relationships for example, soothing tensions, remembering details and keeping peace- often expected of women without recognition.

Gaslighting
A form of manipulation where someone makes you question your memory, feelings or sanity, leaving you confused and doubting yourself.

Medical Gaslighting
When healthcare providers dismiss or minimise women's physical symptoms, delaying diagnosis and leaving women unheard.

Invisible Load
The hidden, relentless responsibilities of daily life such as planning, anticipating, caregiving etc, that consume energy but often go unnoticed.

Trigger
A word, smell, sound or situation that brings back painful memories or emotional responses linked to past trauma.

Validation
Recognising and affirming someone's feelings or experiences as real and important, even if you do not fully understand them.

Trauma
The lasting emotional, physical, and spiritual impact of overwhelming harm such as abuse, violence, or loss. Trauma can live in the body long after the event.

Resilience
The ability to endure hardship, adapt, and begin to heal in the face of adversity. Resilience grows through faith, support and hope.

Spiritual & Theological Terms

Lament
Honest grief expressed before God, often in raw prayer or song, as modelled in the Psalms.
"Pour out your heart like water before the Lord." - Lamentations 2:19

Redemption
God's act of rescuing and restoring people through Christ, especially from sin and brokenness.
"In him we have redemption through his blood." - Ephesians 1:7

Repentance
Turning away from sin with remorse and turning toward God in faith and trust.
"Repent, then and turn to God." - Acts 3:19

Restoration
God's renewal of what was lost or broken—emotionally, spiritually, and relationally.
"Restore to me the joy of your salvation." - Psalm 51:12

Sanctification
The lifelong process of being made holy through God's Spirit, becoming more like Christ.
"It is God's will that you should be sanctified." - 1 Thessalonians 4:3

Shame
A deep sense of unworthiness or "not being enough," often rooted in past experiences, abuse, or cultural stigma.
"There is now no condemnation for those who are in Christ Jesus." - Romans 8:1

Silent Struggles
Inner battles of the mind, body, or spirit that women keep hidden due to fear, stigma, or lack of safe support.
"Come to me, all who are weary and burdened, and I will give you rest." - Matthew 11:28

Silenced Submission
The misuse of scripture or culture to suppress women's voices and agency, rather than teaching the biblical model of mutual love.

Spiritual Bypassing
Using spiritual words or practices to avoid facing real emotional pain for example, saying "just pray more" instead of addressing trauma.
"He gives strength to the weary and increases the power of the weak." - Isaiah 40:29

Wholeness
The state of living in restored identity; emotionally, spiritually and physically, where wounds no longer define a woman's worth.
"May your whole spirit, soul and body be kept blameless at the coming of our Lord Jesus Christ." - 1 Thessalonians 5:23

BIBLIOGRAPHY

Acknowledgement of Sources: *Every effort has been made to acknowledge and reference all sources accurately and fully. Any omissions or errors are unintentional; corrections are welcome in future editions.*

Biblical References

- Aland, Kurt, et al. *The Greek New Testament.* Stuttgart: Deutsche Bibelgesellschaft, 2012.
- Brown, F., Driver, S. R., & Briggs, C. A. *Hebrew and English Lexicon of the Old Testament.* Oxford: Clarendon Press, 1979.
- Holy Bible, English Standard Version. Wheaton, IL: Crossway, 2016.
- Holy Bible, New International Version. Grand Rapids, MI: Zondervan, 2011.
- Holy Bible, New Revised Standard Version. New York: HarperCollins, 1989.

Academic and Theological Works

- Allender, Dan B. *The Wounded Heart: Hope for Adult Victims of Childhood Sexual Abuse.* Colorado Springs: NavPress, 2008.

- Bonhoeffer, Dietrich. *Life Together.* New York: Harper & Row, 1954.
- Brown, Brené. *The Gifts of Imperfection.* Center City: Hazelden, 2010.
- Custis James, Carolyn. *Half the Church: Recapturing God's Global Vision for Women.* Grand Rapids: Zondervan, 2011.
- Felker Jones, Beth. *God's Many Splendored Image: Theological Anthropology for Christian Formation.* Grand Rapids: Baker Academic, 2010.
- Grenz, Stanley J., & Kjesbo, Denise Muir. *Women in the Church: A Biblical Theology of Women in Ministry.* Downers Grove: InterVarsity Press, 1995.
- Nouwen, Henri J. M. *The Wounded Healer.* New York: Image Books, 1979.
- Plantinga, Cornelius. *Not the Way It's Supposed to Be: A Breviary of Sin.* Grand Rapids: Eerdmans, 1995.
- Storkey, Elaine. *Scars Across Humanity: Understanding and Overcoming Violence Against Women.* London: SPCK, 2015.
- Trible, Phyllis. Texts of Terror: *Literary-Feminist Readings of Biblical Narratives.* Philadelphia: Fortress Press, 1984.
- Tutu, Desmond. *No Future Without Forgiveness.* New York: Doubleday, 1999.
- Wright, N. T. *Surprised by Hope.* New York: HarperOne, 2008.

Medical and Counselling Sources

- American Psychiatric Association. *Diagnostic and Statistical Manual of Mental Disorders (DSM-5)*. Arlington, VA: APA, 2013.
- Burns, David. *Feeling Good: The New Mood Therapy.* New York: HarperCollins, 1999.
- Corey, Gerald. *Theory and Practice of Counselling and Psychotherapy.* Belmont, CA: Cengage, 2017.
- Crichton, Charles. "Endometriosis: Pathophysiology and Management." *British Journal of Obstetrics and Gynaecology* 124, no. 3 (2017): 283–289.
- Herman, Judith. *Trauma and Recovery: The Aftermath of Violence.* New York: Basic Books, 2015 (Updated Edition).
- Langberg, Diane. *Suffering and the Heart of God: How Trauma Destroys and Christ Restores.* Greensboro: New Growth Press, 2015.
- McMinn, Mark. *Psychology, Theology, and Spirituality in Christian Counselling.* Carol Stream: Tyndale, 2011.
- van der Kolk, Bessel. *The Body Keeps the Score: Brain, Mind, and Body in the Healing of Trauma.* New York: Viking, 2014.
- Yalom, Irvin. *Existential Psychotherapy.* New York: Basic Books, 1980.

Journals and Articles

- *American Journal of Psychiatry.* Various issues, 2010–2023.
- *British Medical Journal (BMJ).* Women's Health & Reproductive Studies, 2008–2022.
- *Journal of Psychology and Christianity.* Issues on pastoral and clinical counselling.
- *The Lancet.* Series on Violence Against Women and Girls, 2014–2021.
- Smith, Jane. "Faith and Female Mental Health: Bridging Clinical and Pastoral Gaps." *Journal of Pastoral Care & Counselling,* 2019.

Cultural, Social, and Legal Sources

- African Women's Development Fund. *Voice and Visibility: Women's Experiences in Africa.* Accra: AWDF, 2017.
- Amnesty International. *The State of the World's Human Rights.* London: Amnesty, 2022.
- Crenshaw, Kimberlé. "Mapping the Margins: Intersectionality, Identity Politics, and Violence Against Women of Color." *Stanford Law Review* 43, no. 6 (1991): 1241–1299.
- Dube, Musa W. *Postcolonial Feminist Interpretation of the Bible.* St. Louis: Chalice Press, 2000.
- Equality and Human Rights Commission (UK). *Pregnancy and Maternity-Related Discrimination and Disadvantage.* London: EHRC, 2016.

- Oduyoye, Mercy Amba. *Daughters of Anowa: African Women and Patriarchy.* Maryknoll: Orbis Books, 1995.
- Office for National Statistics (UK). *Domestic Abuse in England and Wales: Year Ending 2022.* London: ONS, 2023.
- Phiri, Isabel Apawo, and Sarojini Nadar, eds. *African Women, Religion, and Health: Essays in Honor of Mercy Amba Ewudziwa Oduyoye.* Maryknoll: Orbis Books, 2006.
- World Health Organization. *Violence Against Women: Key Facts.* Geneva: WHO, 2021.

SCRIPTURE INDEX

Old Testament

- **Genesis 16:13** – Hagar names God "El Roi," the God who sees.
- **Exodus 3:7** – God hears the cries of His people.
- **Deuteronomy 10:18** – God defends the widow and orphan.
- **Job 3–5** – Job curses the day of his birth.
- **Psalm 9:9** – The Lord is a refuge for the oppressed.
- **Psalm 23:1–3** – The Lord is my shepherd; He restores my soul.
- **Psalm 31:9–10** – A psalm of anguish and sorrow.
- **Psalm 34:5** – Those who look to Him are radiant.
- **Psalm 34:18** – The Lord is close to the brokenhearted.
- **Psalm 56:8** – God collects our tears.
- **Psalm 68:5** – God as defender of widows.
- **Psalm 92:12–14** – The righteous still bear fruit in old age.
- **Psalm 113:9** – God settles the childless woman in her home.
- **Psalm 139:14** – Fearfully and wonderfully made.
- **Psalm 146:9** – The Lord sustains the widow and fatherless.
- **Psalm 147:3** – He heals the brokenhearted.
- **Proverbs 14:13** – Even in laughter the heart may ache.

- **Proverbs 16:31** – Gray hair is a crown of splendour.
- **Proverbs 22:6** – Train up a child in the way he should go.
- **Proverbs 31:8-9** – Speak up for those who cannot speak for themselves.
- **Ecclesiastes 3:1** – To everything there is a season.
- **Ecclesiastes 3:4** – A time to weep and a time to laugh.
- **Ecclesiastes 3:7** – A time to be silent and a time to speak.
- **Isaiah 30:15** – In quietness and trust is your strength.
- **Isaiah 40:11** – God gently leads mothers with young children.
- **Isaiah 40:29** – He gives strength to the weary.
- **Isaiah 42:3** – A bruised reed He will not break.
- **Isaiah 43:4** – You are precious and honoured in My sight.
- **Isaiah 46:4** – God sustains even in old age.
- **Isaiah 58:10** – Spend yourselves on behalf of the hungry.
- **Isaiah 61:1** – To bind up the brokenhearted.
- **Jeremiah 1:5** – Before I formed you, I knew you.
- **Jeremiah 29:11** – Plans to prosper and not to harm.
- **Lamentations 2:19** – Pour out your heart like water before the Lord.
- **Lamentations 3:22-23** – God's mercies are new every morning.
- **Amos 5:24** – Let justice roll like waters.
- **Micah 6:8** – Act justly, love mercy, walk humbly.

New Testament

- **Matthew 5:4** – Blessed are those who mourn.
- **Matthew 6:34** – Do not worry about tomorrow.
- **Matthew 11:28** – Come to Me, all who are weary.
- **Matthew 27:46** – My God, why have You forsaken me?
- **Mark 6:31** – Come away and rest.
- **Luke 1:38** – Mary's submission to God's call.
- **Luke 5:16** – Jesus withdrew to lonely places and prayed.
- **Luke 8:43–48** – The woman with the issue of blood.
- **Luke 10:39–42** – Mary of Bethany sits at Jesus' feet.
- **Luke 22:44** – Jesus sweats blood in Gethsemane.
- **John 4:26–29** – The Samaritan woman at the well.
- **John 8:7** – Let him who is without sin cast the first stone.
- **John 8:11** – Neither do I condemn you.
- **John 11:35** – Jesus wept with Mary and Martha.
- **John 14:27** – My peace I give you.
- **Acts 2:42–47** – Early church sharing burdens.
- **Romans 8:1** – No condemnation for those in Christ.
- **1 Corinthians 6:19–20** – Your body is a temple of the Holy Spirit.
- **1 Corinthians 7:7, 34** – Singleness as a gift.
- **1 Corinthians 14:34** – Women should remain silent (misapplied text).
- **2 Corinthians 12:9** – My grace is sufficient for you.
- **Ephesians 4:15** – Speak the truth in love.
- **Ephesians 5:11** – Have nothing to do with fruitless deeds of darkness.

- **Ephesians 5:21–25** – Mutual submission and love.
- **Ephesians 6:1–3** – Children obey your parents.
- **Philippians 4:11** – Content in every circumstance.
- **Colossians 2:10** – You are complete in Him.
- **Colossians 3:23** – Work with all your heart, as for the Lord.
- **1 Thessalonians 4:3** – God's will is your sanctification.
- **1 Thessalonians 5:23** – May your whole spirit, soul and body be kept blameless.
- **1 Timothy 5:18** – The labourer deserves wages.
- **Titus 2:3–5** – Older women to teach the younger.
- **1 Peter 3:1–3, 7** – Wives and husbands, mutual honour.
- **1 Peter 5:7** – Cast all your anxiety on Him.
- **1 John 4:18** – Perfect love drives out fear.
- **Revelation 21:4** – God will wipe every tear.

ABOUT THE AUTHOR

 Dr. Olivia Winner is a Christian counsellor, author and speaker with more than two decades of experience walking alongside women, families and church communities. She holds a PhD in Christian Counselling with a specialisation in marriage, families and child therapy, and has served in both the United Kingdom and Africa, offering pastoral and professional care to women across cultures.

As the founder and director of The Winners Female Family Organization, Dr. Winner has dedicated her life to giving voice to women's unspoken struggles, supporting those navigating trauma, reproductive grief, emotional labour, leadership pressures and faith challenges. Her work integrates clinical insight with biblical wisdom, helping women rediscover their worth, their voice and their freedom in Christ.

Born in Uganda and now based in the UK, Dr. Winner brings a unique perspective shaped by both African heritage and global experience. Her writing and counselling reflect deep cultural sensitivity, theological depth and a compassionate understanding of the hidden burdens that women carry.

Dr. Winner is also a wife and mother, drawing from her own journey of balancing faith, family and vocation. Her pastoral heart, professional expertise and lived experience combine to create a voice that is both tender and strong calling women out of silence and into healing.

This book, **Whispers of the Heart: Exploring the Silent Struggles of Women Through Christian Counselling and Family Therapy**, is her invitation to women everywhere to know that they are seen, heard and loved by God.

Veridian Christian University - PhD in Christian Counselling, Marriage, Families and Child Therapy

Prescribing - University of Essex

Minor illness and injuries/ Emergency Nurse Practitioner - University of Greenwich

Clinical Assessment Certification - The university of Anglia Ruskin

Adult Nursing - University of West London

www.ingramcontent.com/pod-product-compliance
Lightning Source LLC
Chambersburg PA
CBHW051605010526
44119CB00056B/791